The Extinct and Endangered Animal Cookbook

Also by Michael Westerfield

The Language of Crows
The Road to the Poorhouse

The Extinct and Endangered Animal Cookbook

How Human Appetites are Creating a New Age of Extinction

Michael Westerfield

ASHFORD PRESS

Ashford Press
P.O. Box 513
Willimantic, CT 06226

Printed in the United States of America
First Edition

ISBN: 978-0-937992-05-0

Library of Congress Control Number: 2019914429

Cover Design: June Westerfield, juneofallthings.com

Author Photograph: Anna Duprey

All illustrations other than the author photograph
are in the Public Domain.

For all those who have worked so many years
to preserve and restore our environment
and
for the millions more who are joining in
to complete the great work

Contents

NOTE: Recipes included in this book are for informational purposes only. Please do not attempt to prepare them at home, even in the unlikely event that you could obtain the necessary ingredients.

Take just enough.

1. Devouring the Planet

In 1859, Peter Lund Simmons authored *The Curiosities of Food*, the first attempt at producing a comprehensive study of items eaten by humans the world over. In his Preliminary Remarks he commented on the "omnivorous propensities" of the human species.

If animals could speak, as Aesop and other fabulists make them seem to do, they would declare man to be the most voracious animal in existence. There is scarcely any living thing that flies in the air, swims in the sea, or moves on land, that is not made to minister to his appetite in some region or other.

Simmons goes on to list a vast number of organisms that humans feed upon, from monkeys eaten in South America to sea slug soup in China, all of them created by God for our consumption.

Rich provision has been made for his [man's] tastes, making glad the fields, the meadows, the vineyards, the orchards, the waters. And the air, peopled as they are with things made to be quartered, and cooked, and eaten.... The Creator granted to the use of Man animal food as well as every green herb. Whatsoever is sold in the shambles [meat market] and is set before you eat, therefore, asking no questions for conscience sake.

In those days, all god given resources were seen as infinitely renewable and, for the most part, with the exception of mineral deposits, they actually were. If wisely managed by a reasonably sized human population, there was no particular reason why the cycle of nature could not go on unbroken indefinitely, barring the occasional gigantic natural catastrophe.

What Simmons' view of a beneficent God providing for the needs of humanity did not take into account was that our continual development of technology would allow us to capture, kill, and harvest living things with incredible efficiency and to dramatically modify the environment to provide ever increasing quantities of fewer and fewer varieties of "foodstuffs" to satisfy the appetites of an endlessly expanding population. It is the combination of these two factors, together with our chronic inability to consume resources within sustainable limits, which has made us the greatest threat that has ever been posed by a single species to life on this planet.

As of this writing, the human population has burgeoned far beyond a reasonable size – 7.7 billion and counting – and our profligate consumption of the planet's resources has been anything but wise. It is calculated that we are using up the Earth's resources 1.75 times faster than its ecosystem can regenerate.

One of the most significant unintended consequence of uncontrolled human consumption is the extinction of numerous other species. Native animals and plants are either devoured [completely out of existence] directly as food or their environments are so dramatically altered that they can no longer survive "in the wild." This process appears to have been going on for as long as humans have utilized tools to obtain food, and has accelerated with each advance in technology. It has recently been calculated that the current rate of extinction is 1,000 times higher than pre-human levels, amounting to about 900 species a year, and rising rapidly.

So dramatic has our effect been on the environment that we are believed to have entered the Anthropocene Age, a new epoch in the history of the earth where virtually everything we see, hear, feel, eat or drink has been shaped, directly or indirectly, by human hands and minds. The very climate of the planet has been altered by our unsustainable consumption of animal, vegetable, and mineral resources, with terrible consequences which we are only just beginning to understand. One thing, however, is clear; there is no time left for procrastination. Our actions in the next few years will determine for thousands of years to come both the fate of humanity and of millions of other species with whom we share Earth's marvelous, but increasingly fragile ecosystem.

In order to decide how we must act in order to minimize the disastrous effects of the developing ecosystem collapse, it is vital to understand how we arrived at our unsustainable present. No single action, no great meteor collision or volcanic eruption brought about our new age of extinction. The recipes in this book were selected to illustrate some of the ways in which our habits of thoughtless consumption have devastated species diversity on our planet. The recipes are genuine, even the most bizarre sounding ones. Whale croquettes really were recommended by the U.S. Bureau of Fisheries and a famous Chinese chef just recently stirred up a storm of controversy by cutting up and cooking an endangered giant salamander live on TV.

It is my hope that by reviewing our culinary excesses of the past, we can learn how the choices that a few generations of people make in something as small as deciding what to have for dinner can make or break a planet.

2. Discovering Extinction

Charles Willson Peale's 1806 painting, *The Exhumation of the Mastodon*, presents a somewhat exaggerated picture of the excavation of a nearly complete skeleton of a mastodon near Newberg, New York, in 1801. Peale, who is best known for his life portraits of George Washington, Thomas Jefferson, Benjamin Franklin and other leading figures of the American Revolution, created a public portrait gallery in his own Philadelphia home in 1782. Over time, he began a collection of "curiosities" which he exhibited in what grew into one of the earliest natural history museums. It was in his dual capacity as artist and naturalist that he directed the excavation of the Newberg mammoth and ultimately exhibited the mounted skeleton in his Philadelphia museum. Institutions like Peale's were at the forefront of a revolution in science that would forever change our view of the natural world.

Although humans had been hunting and eating animals into extinction for many thousands of years, until fairly recently no one had actually noticed that animals which were once plentiful no longer existed. This was largely due to the fact that our world view was local rather than global; for most humans the range of their personal experience might have been only a few miles, or a few hundred miles, at most. Animals came and went, and if they weren't in the tribe's home territory, why then they must have been somewhere else.

It was also the Christian belief that God had created the world as a perfect whole, a web of life in which every creature in existence also had existed throughout all of the past and would continue to do so until the very end of the world. This belief was so deeply ingrained that the extinction of a species was simply inconceivable. Although the disappearance of various species was noted in the historical record, and their absence from the dining table was apparent, the significance of the information was not recognized until many years after the fact.

Aurochs

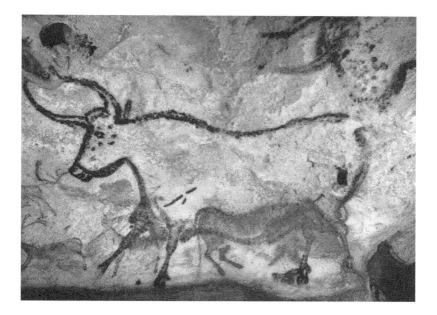

Of all the animals that have gone extinct since the appearance of *Homo sapiens,* it is probable that none has contributed more to our present day diet than the Aurochs, *Bos taurus primigenius,* the ancestor of all domestic cattle. Wild aurochs were significantly larger than current breeds and were widespread throughout Europe, Asia and North Africa. They were hunted by Neanderthals, with wooden spears, depicted by Cro-Magnon Man on cave walls at Lascaux, and revered by Minoans who left frescos of slender youths leaping over the horns of huge bulls in their palaces on Crete. Around 50 B.C.E., Julius Caesar wrote about the Aurochs in Germany in his account of *The Gallic Wars.*

These are a little below the elephant in size, and of the appearance, colour, and shape of a bull. Their strength and speed are extraordinary; they spare neither man nor wild beast which they have espied. These the Germans take with much pains [trapping them]in pits and kill[ing] them. The young men harden themselves with this exercise, and practice themselves in this kind of hunting, and those who have slain the greatest number of them, having produced the horns in public, to serve as evidence, receive great praise. But not even when taken very young can they be rendered familiar to men and tamed. The size, shape, and appearance of their horns differ much from the horns of our oxen. These they anxiously seek after, and bind at the tips with silver, and use as cups at their most sumptuous entertainments.

It is uncertain whether Caesar ever actually saw an aurochs in Gaul, though at times they were featured in spectacles in Rome and elsewhere in the Empire. They clearly were not close to the size of an African elephant, being more in the range of about 6 feet at the shoulder, with horns that could reach 3 feet in length. Even by Caesar's day they had disappeared from much of their range, as agriculture advanced into the once densely forested areas. Unrestricted hunting also thinned their numbers since they had the misfortune to always be cast in the role of trophy animals to be slain by hunters as a test of skill and bravery. Diseases spread by the ever increasing number of domestic cattle also took their toll on the mighty Aurochs.

By the 1600s, the species existed only in the remnants of the ancient forests of Poland, where they continued to be hunted for sport by the nobility. The last aurochs bull died in 1620. Its horns were preserved and highly ornamented for ceremonial drinking purposes and remain on exhibit in the Armory Museum [*Livrustkammaren*] in the Royal Palace in Stockholm, Sweden.

The very last member of the species, a cow, died from natural causes in a Polish forest in 1627. It was the world's first recorded extinction, although it was not recognized as such at the time.

RECIPES:

There appears to be only one recorded "recipe" for cooking aurochs that was written by someone who might actually have had experience dealing with the beast in a kitchen, Marx Rumpolt, the head cook to the Elector of Mainz, Daniel Brendel of Homburg. In 1581, he wrote *Ein new Kochbuch* [*A New Cookbook*], which contained many hundreds of "recipes," some much more detailed than others. His brief comments on cooking aurochs come in a section on cooking wild game.

It is also possible to cook an aurochs, as one would an ox, except that an aurochs is larger, and when one takes it to roast, one must salt it, and the meat is good cooked in stew like other beef. It can be cooked dark or rare, as one might have it.

Given Rumpoldt's comments and the fact that it is the ancestor of all modern cattle, it seems reasonable to assume that aurochs could be substituted in all recipes calling for beef.

CONSERVATION STATUS: EXTINCT

For a number of years there have been on-going efforts to recreate living aurochs. The theory is, that since it is the sole ancestor of all living cattle, it is highly probable that the genes that made aurochs distinct are still present in the various modern breeds of cattle. This being the case, it should be possible by selective breeding, and/or by genetic engineering, to recreate the ancestor species.

In the 1920s an effort was made by Heinz and Lutz Heck, both zoo directors in Germany, to resurrect the aurochs by cross breeding modern varieties of cattle, selecting for specific visible characteristics of their ancestor, size, color, horn shape and so on. The result was the production of "Heck Cattle," considered to be an "effigy" breed, one closely resembling the aurochs in appearance but not necessarily identical in genetic makeup. Since then there have been numerous attempts made to recreate the aurochs using various methods including obtaining DNA from preserved museum specimens as well as gene sequencing and editing. Given this widespread obsession and the innovative techniques and resources being focused on the aurochs, it seems quite possible that the first species observed to have gone extinct might turn out to also be the first to be resurrected. In short, the prognosis is quite good for the ultimate production of at least a near replica of the original animal.

Dodo

The Dodo has long been the "poster child" of extinct animals. Its absurd name and bizarre appearance caught the popular imagination, particularly after it made a cameo appearance in Lewis Carroll's book *Alice in Wonderland*, illustrated by John Tenniel. It is ironic, that in *Alice*, the Dodo holds a race in which everyone wins, while in the real world he was one of the earliest recognized losers in what now appears to be a planetary race to extinction.

The Dodo, along with a number of other distinctive species, including a variety of giant tortoise, was endemic to Mauritius, an island off the African coast to the east of Madagascar. It was a large, flightless bird that stood about 3 feet high and is estimated to have weighed between 29 and 51 pounds. It had evolved in isolation on the island in the absence of predators and lost the ability to fly as it increased in body mass.

One of the earliest written accounts, from a 1598 journal, describes the bird as follows:

Blue parrots are very numerous there, as well as other birds; among which are a kind, conspicuous for their size, larger than our swans, with huge heads only half covered with skin as if clothed with a hood. These birds lack wings, in the place of which 3 or 4 blackish feathers protrude. The tail consists of a few soft incurved feathers, which are ash coloured. These we used to call 'Walghvogel' [wooden bird?], for the reason that the longer and oftener they were cooked, the less soft and more insipid eating they became. Nevertheless their belly and breast were of a pleasant flavour and easily masticated.

In 1634, Sir Thomas Herbert (who had visited Mauritius in 1627) described the dodo in his book *A Relation of Some Yeares Travaille into Afrique and the Greater Asia*:

Her body is round and fat, few weigh less than fifty pound. It is reputed more for wonder than for food, greasie stomackes may seeke after them, but to the delicate they are offensive and of no nourishment. Her visage darts forth melancholy, as sensible of Nature's injurie in framing so great a body to be guided with complementall wings, so small and impotent, that they serve only to prove her bird. The halfe of her head is naked seeming couered with a fine vaile, her bill is crooked downwards, in midst is the trill [nostril], from which part to the end tis a light green, mixed with pale yellow tincture; her eyes are small and like to Diamonds, rund and rowling; her clothing downy feathers, her train three small plumes, short and inproportionable, her legs suiting her body, her pounces sharpe, her appetite strong and greedy. Stones and iron are digested, which description will better be conceived in her representation.

Like virtually all descriptions of wildlife by early seafarers and adventurers, those of the Dodo contain an evaluation of its suitability as food. In the days before any form of food preservation beyond salting, pickling and drying, fresh food supplies were constantly required on any extended voyage. Passing ships would fill their larders with anything edible that they could kill, capture or harvest from any place they might drop anchor. Large species, that had evolved in the absence of predators, such as the Dodo and the giant tortoises of Mauritius, were particularly vulnerable.

In addition to the depredations of ships' crews, the Dutch made several generally unsuccessful attempts at colonization and exploitation of the island from 1598 through 1710. More than once, colonists were left abandoned and forced to live off the land, eating up the local resources. They also intentionally or accidentally introduced non-native species. In those days, it was the general practices for ship's crews visiting new territories to leave behind European food animals, such as goats, pigs and chickens, in the hope that they would reproduce and provide supplies for future visitors. Destructive species such as domestic cats and ship's rats were accidentally introduced and these could play havoc with ground nesting species such as the dodo.

Generally, the main purpose of establishing colonies in the remote areas of the world was to exploit them commercially. On Mauritius, the natural groves of ebony trees had first attracted mercantile ventures, and later large areas were cleared for sugar cane production. The habitat loss resulting from the desire for the beautiful black wood, and the thirst for rum made from cane molasses, finished off most of the endemic species that humans did not eat.

The dodo passed from discovery to extinction so quickly that very few specimens made it back to Europe, and it was commonly considered to be a mythical animal. A quantity of dodo bones have been found over the years, from which the reconstructions of the bird in museums have been made, but the only known samples of "soft tissue" are the preserved head and one foot kept at the Oxford University Museum of Natural History.

RECIPES:

It appears that dodos used for food were either roasted on spits or boiled, generally by pretty desperate men who could capture nothing better to eat. One remarkable "seasoning" that was recommended, was to improve the flavor of dodo by basting it with the fat from a species of giant tortoise, which is also extinct, but which flourished on Mauritius at the time of the dodo.

STATUS: EXTINCT

Given the dodo's prominent status both in the history of extinction and in the public mind, along with the advances in genetic engineering, it is only logical that it would be considered a top candidate for efforts at "de-extinction." The dodo's genome has recently been completely sequenced, which greatly improves the chances of the species' resurrection. It also has a relatively close relative, the Nicobar Pigeon which, although endangered, has been successfully bred in captivity and might prove useful as a source of genetic material that could be "edited" to match that of the dodo.

It should be noted that the Island of Mauritius is a leader in the field of the rescue of critically endangered species and there is great interest there in resurrecting the island's most famous character. It does appear that if de-extinction is at all possible, then the dodo might be one of the first species to rise again from the dead.

Steller's Sea Cow

The above drawing, made by Friedrich Plenisner, is the only illustration of Steller's Sea Cow known to have been drawn from an actual specimen. Within 27 years of its "discovery," it suffered the not uncommon fate of being eaten into extinction by explorers, adventurers and sailors.

Shortly before his death in 1725, Tsar Peter the Great of Russia authorized a vast plan of exploration of the lands bordering the Pacific Basin, including the Artic North and the coast of North America. This venture, later known as the Great Northern Expedition, evolved into what was possibly the greatest exploratory venture in history, spanning ten years, involving over 3,000 people, with an international team of scientists and scholars from Russia, Germany, France and Sweden. It would not be unreasonable to say there was nothing comparable to it in cost and complexity until the race to conquer space in the 1960s.

Among the participants in one of the phases of the expedition was a German volunteer "adjunct," Georg Wilhelm Steller, who joined Vitus Bering in 1740 to take part in the exploration of the area between Siberia and North America. Steller's adventures and exploits are too numerous to mention, beyond the fact that he was the first non-native to set foot in Alaska and that he discovered six previously unknown species, including a gigantic relative of the dugong and manatee, later named Steller's Sea Cow, and the well-known Steller's Jay. The jay is the only one of the six species that is not now extinct or endangered.

The illustration below, which is a 1925 recreation, by Loenhard Stejneger, of the scene of Steller measuring a sea cow, gives a fairly accurate idea of the animal's size.

Virtually all expeditions, until recently, expected to "live off the land," and the one Steller was on was was no exception. When shipwrecked upon Bering Island, "which lies in the channel between America and Asia," the flesh of the sea otter was their principle food and one which Steller credited with saving the men from scurvy. A real bounty of food, however, was provided by a female "manatee" or "sea cow," which was killed on July 12, 1742. This animal was measured to be 296 inches in length [24.66 feet] and estimated to weigh 8,000 pounds.

At least three others were killed, and all were dissected and examined by Steller and the results carefully noted for later publication. Like almost all early descriptions of newly discovered animals, aside from anatomy and behavior, that of the Sea Cow also includes a lengthy description of its suitability as food. Fat often seems to be an obsession with these explorers, but that was because it was, along with fresh fruit and vegetables, the item most often lacking in their shipboard diet of salted meat and "hardtack" bread. Steller notes in his *De bestiis marinis [The Beasts of the Sea]*,

The fat underlies the cuticle and skin and covers the whole body to the depth of a span, and in some parts is almost 9 inches thick...when exposed to the sun it becomes yellow like May butter. Its odor and flavor are so agreeable that it can not be compared with the fat of any other sea beast. Indeed, it is by far preferable to that of any other quadruped....When tried out it is so sweet and fine flavored that we lost all desire for butter....And, indeed, its use as medicine is not to be despised, for it moves the bowels gently, producing no loss of appetite or nausea, even when drunk from a cup...

The flesh has a grain somewhat tougher and coarser than beef, and is redder than the flesh of land animals...Although the flesh needs to be cooked longer, yet when done has an excellent taste, not easy to distinguish from that of beef...

A full-grown animal weighs about 8,000 pounds... There is so large a number of these animals about this island that they would suffice to support all the inhabitants of Kamchatka.

In this last statement, Steller was quite mistaken. Although these sea cows were quite widespread along the Pacific rim before the Ice Age, by the time of the Great Northern Expedition there was only a single remnant population remaining in the area of Bering Island, which was quickly eaten into extinction by the flood of explorers and fur trappers that followed in the expedition's wake.

Aside from the human appetite for food, the huge profits to be made from trapping and selling the skins of the sea otters, which were present in great abundance in the home territory of the sea cow, played a significant part in the demise of the giant sea mammal. Sea otters eat sea urchins which eat the kelp which was also the primary food of Steller's sea cow. It is postulated that removing huge number of sea otters allowed the population of sea urchins to explode and very rapidly destroy the kelp beds upon which the sea cows relied for sustenance. Thus, both used for food and deprived of nourishment, Steller's Sea Cow quite possibly set the record for the shortest time between discovery and total extinction.

RECIPES:

None other than boiling and presumably roasting.

CONSERVATION STATUS: EXTINCT

Steller's Sea Cow is unlikely to be the subject of attempts to recreate the species. There may be no extant tissue samples from which DNA could be extracted or a genome determined, although bones have been found and are exhibited in various museums, including a relatively complete skeleton at the Finish Museum of Natural History. There have been sporadic, unconfirmed reports of sightings of the sea cows as recently as the 1960s in the Kamchatka in the far northeast of Russia.

Sea Otter

The Sea Otter, *Enhydra lutris,* is the largest member of the weasel family, growing to about four feet in length and weighing up to 100 pounds. Historically, its population may have numbered more than a million individuals spread in shallow coastal waters around the North Pacific from Japan, up the coast of Siberia to the Aleutian Islands and down the coast of North America to southern California. The Sea Otter is distinguished by having the densest fur of any animal, which has made their pelts tremendously sought after in the fur trade. They also, apparently, make very good eating.

The commercial value of the Sea Otter first came to the attention of Europeans during the course of the Russian Great Northern Expedition. While stranded on Bering Island, during the course of that expedition in the early 1840s, Georg

Wilhelm Steller encountered large numbers of sea otters that "covered the shore in great droves." He studied their behavior and anatomy and also killed many hundreds, both for their valuable pelts and for food. He found them to be delicious.

The flesh of the adult otter is much more tender and savory than that of the seal. The flesh of the female is best, for it is fatter and more tender, and the fat lies between little membranes. It is for that reason a little hard. In the case of pregnant mothers, the nearer they are to parturition the fatter they are. In this respect they are different from land animals. The flesh of the young otter is most delicious; it can not easily be distinguished from the flesh of an unweaned lamb, whether roasted or boiled, and the gravy from its preparing, in either way, is most delicious. Otter flesh was our principal food on Bering Island; it was also our universal medicine. By its use we were saved from scurvy, and no one got sick of it, although we ate it every day half raw and without bread. The liver, heart, and kidneys tasted exactly like those of the calf.

Steller's return to civilization with a large cargo of extremely valuable pelts touched off an event that came to be known as the "Great Hunt", a sort of "fur rush" between 1741 and 1911, that reduced the population of the animals to near extinction levels. When most hunting was banned in 1911, perhaps 1,000 or 2,000 individuals were left in a fraction of the species' historic range, with only small remnant populations remaining in remote locations. Since then only a very limited amount of hunting by indigenous peoples has been permitted.

In the 20th Century, conservation efforts, including relocating otters to parts of their previous range, were remarkably successful with the population size worldwide growing to over 100,000.

Despite the remarkable comeback of the sea otter from the brink of extinction, the species is suffering declines in various parts of its range due to a number of factors. In Alaska a dramatic reduction in the number of otters seems to be due to an increase in predation by Orcas, driven to a by a significant decline in other prey species. In California, great white sharks are increasingly preying on sea otters and disease claims a significant percentage of the population. The otters are also particularly vulnerable to oil spills and many hundred have died from that cause in recent years. Environmental degradation due to pollution from agricultural runoff and the effects of climate change also are placing great stress on otter populations. Additionally, commercial fishermen see the otters as competition for their harvests of abalone and red sea urchins and make few efforts to protect them from death by entanglement in fishing gear and sometimes even kill the otters intentionally.

RECIPES

La Varenne's *Le Cuisinier Francois,* first published in 1651, contained more than 800 recipes, two of which were for preparing sea otter for the table.

Sea-Otter in a Court-Bouillon. Dress a sea-otter and prepare it for putting into court-bouillon, which you make up in the same way as for the brill. When it has cooked, serve it dry, with parsley. [Court bullion refers to a simple and quickly made bullion and brill is a flatfish related to the turbot. Sea otters were included in the fish section of the cookbook and could be consumed on days when fasting from meat was required.]

Sea-Otter on the Grill. Dress the sea-otter and roast it. When it is done, make whatever sauce you like for it, provided it tastes strong and, because those large chunks don't readily take on a flavoring, split it or slice it on top. Simmer it in its sauce until it has soaked up almost all of it. Then serve it, garnished with whatever you have on hand.

River otters are still hunted and their meat sold in exotic game markets and served in some specialty restaurants. The following recipe should work equally well for sea otters.

CURRIED OTTER

Remove all connective tissue from the meat, section the meat into thin slices and marinate overnight in two parts ranch dressing and one part Dijon mustard.

Drain the meat.

Melt butter in saucepan, add otter, curry powder to taste, and finely chopped rosemary. Stir over medium heat until otter is thoroughly cooked.

Serve hot over rice.

CONSERVATION STATUS: VULNERABLE

As the over-harvesting of the oceans continues, pollution remains unabated, and the effects of climate change become increasingly severe, it can be expected that the sea otter will become increasingly endangered throughout most of its range, and possibly locally extinct in some areas. What is fortunate is that the species does quite well in captivity and is particularly popular as a zoo attraction due to its "cute" appearance and endearing habits. It is therefore likely that many captive populations will be available to once again repopulate traditional areas of their range if ever the current threats are eliminated and enough time passes for ecosystems to recover.

Galapagos Tortoises

By all accounts, giant tortoises are delicious, no matter how you cook them. Explorers, whalers, pirates, naval captains, and even Charles Darwin, described them in their logs and journals as the finest meat they ever ate. Tortoise livers were considered especially delightful.

Although giant tortoises were once found on every continent except Australia and Antarctica, they were unable to adapt to the conditions of the last ice age. By the beginning of the European "Age of Exploration" in the 1500s, they occurred only on a number of relatively small islands off the coasts of Africa and South America. It is possible that at that time, there were several hundred thousand individuals belonging to a number of different species scattered throughout the Galapagos Islands, off the coast of Chile, off the east coast of Africa, on the islands of Mauritius, Reunion, and Rodriguez, as well as three islands in Seychelles, and the remote coralline atoll of Aldabra. Today they are found only in the Galapagos Islands and on Aldabra.

In the 1680s British pirate, William Dampier, visited the Galapagos Islands and noted,

The land-turtles are here so numerous, that five or six hundred men might subsist on them alone for several months, without any other sort of provision: they are extraordinarily large and fat, and so sweet, that no pullet eats more pleasantly.

In 1691, Francois Leguat wrote of the giant tortoises of Rodriguez island,

The flesh is very wholesome, and tastes something like mutton. The fat is extremely white, and never congeals or rises in your stomach, eat as much as you will of it. We all unanimously agreed, 'twas better than the best butter in Europe. To anoint one's self with this oil is an excellent remedy for surfeits, colds, cramps, and several other distempers. The liver of this animal is extraordinarily delicate, 'tis so delicious that one may say of it, it always carries its own sauce with it, dress it how you will.... There are such a plenty of land-turtles in this isle, that sometimes you see two or three thousand in a flock.

In 1835, during his famous visit to the Galapagos Islands, Darwin noted,

While staying in this upper region [of James Island] we lived entirely upon tortoise-meat: the breastplate roasted, with the flesh on it, is very good; and the young tortoises make excellent soup.

Aside from being delicious, the giant tortoises suffered from one other attribute that sealed their fate – they could survive for long periods of time, possibly years, without requiring food or water. This feature allowed seafarers to collect dozens, or even hundreds, of them for a convenient source of food during long voyages. They would simply be allowed to walk around the deck or be stored in the hold, to be slaughtered and eaten fresh as needed.

The African islands which, with the exception of remote Aldabra, lay on main trade routes saw their tortoise populations eaten into extinction even before they could be studied and described in detail. Those in the Galapagos survived largely in isolation until the boom in whaling along the Pacific Coast of South America, starting in the late 1700s, brought hordes of hungry seafarers to their shores. Dozens of ships stocked up on giant tortoises to replenish their food stores for their whale hunts that often lasted for years. In addition, non-native, invasive species which they brought with them, rats, pigs, dogs and cats, devoured the eggs and vulnerable young tortoises.

Even the *Beagle*, when it sailed on its long journey back to England, carried several giant tortoises for food. It wasn't until Darwin was back at home that he realized that he had eaten his most important specimens.

It is quite possible that Galapagos tortoises might have been eaten into extinction, except for one seemingly unrelated event. In 1859, Colonel Edwin L. Drake struck oil in Titusville, Pennsylvania. The petroleum boom very quickly eliminated the need for costly and difficult to obtain whale oil products, and the whaling fleets with their voracious crews rapidly declined from several thousand ships to a mere handful. The last existing wooden whaling ship that frequented the Galapagos Islands is the Charles W. Morgan, a restored museum ship docked in Mystic, Connecticut.

RECIPES:

There appear to be no existing recipes specifically for Galapagos tortoise, presumably because they were primarily eaten by the inhabitants of remote islands and by the crews of long distance sailing ships, neither of whom went in for gourmet cooking.

Mention is made in various records of roasting the flesh, and using it in soups and stews. The fat, apparently, was used like butter and medicinally. Additionally, tortoise eggs were commonly dug up and eaten.

CONSERVATION STATUS: VULNERABLE

PROGNOSIS: Against all odds, a number of species of Galapagos tortoise have survived and are reported to be increasing in number thanks, to protection from hunters and introduced predators, largely through the work of the Galapagos Conservancy. This organization, which has worked for years under extremely difficult conditions, collects eggs and hatchlings from natural nests and rears them for several years before releasing them into their present or former habitats. Of the fifteen identified species and/or subspecies of tortoises, currently six are considered Critically Endangered, three Endangered, three Vulnerable, and two Extinct. A third species went extinct in the mid-1800s but never was officially described or named.

One additional species exists on the Aldabra Atoll in the Seychelles. This species, because of the remote location of its home, and a long history of active conservation work, actually has succeeded not only in avoiding extinction, but of maintaining healthy population of around 100,000. It is none-the-less considered to be "vulnerable" due to the effects of a warming climate, such as rising sea level eroding the low, sandy atoll on which they live and increasingly frequent droughts reducing the already limited water supplies.

Most recently a new and dire threat to giant tortoises has arisen in the form of an insect almost invisible to the naked eye, the little fire ant, or electric ant, *Wasmannia auropunctata*. This 1.5millimeter long invasive species, which has just recently reached the Galapagos and other Pacific Islands, has a powerful sting for its size and feeds on the newly hatched tortoises. It also attacks the eyes and cloacae of the adults. It is considered possibly the most serious ant threat in the area.

HOLOCENE MEGAFAUNA

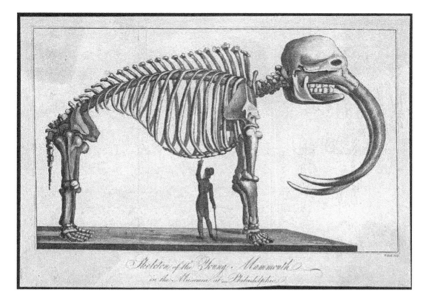

Skeleton of the Young Mammoth in the Museum at Philadelphia

Despite the fact that a number of species, such as the Dodo and Aurochs, had dwindled away completely, with their absence being very publicly noted, the idea that an animal could actually go extinct was largely inconceivable before the 18th Century. It took dramatic evidence that something which clearly could not possibly exist in the present day had, in fact actually existed in the past to shake the foundations of accepted reality. Fortunately, such evidence in the form of skeletons of gigantic elephant-like creatures, mammoths and mastodons, started turning up with remarkable frequency in North America and elsewhere.

The first recorded evidence in America of these massive creatures was a five pound mastodon tooth that was found in the Hudson River Valley 1705 and which was initially mistaken for having belonged to one of the biblical giants which inhabited the earth "in those days." Bones found near the tooth were judged to belong to an unknown being – an *incognitum* – perhaps 60 feet tall. As more gigantic remains turned up elsewhere, it appeared as though huge creatures of all kinds had once lived almost everywhere on earth.

Two of the leading players in the discovery/identification of these previously unknown mega-animals were the French naturalist and zoologist, Jean Léopold Nicolas Frédéric, Baron Cuvier (better known as Georges Cuvier), and the President of the United States, Thomas Jefferson.

Jefferson seems to have been obsessed with studying, identifying and, if possible, finding living specimens of the animals to which the gigantic bones belonged. He routinely had travelers and explorers, including Lewis and Clark, send him any fossil bones they found, and he was reputed to spread them out on the floor of the White House and attempt to assemble them like fantastic puzzles. One set of bones sent to him, that had been found in a cave in what is now West Virginia, were of a previously unknown creature, a giant ground sloth that bears the scientific name *Megalonyx jeffersonii.*

Until close to the end of his life, Jefferson did not believe that any species could become extinct and he thought it probable that somewhere on the vast and poorly explored American continent such creatures still roamed.

If Jefferson was the fanatical amateur naturalist, Georges Cuvier was the consummate professional scientist, a founder of the fields of comparative anatomy and paleontology. He also was the first to firmly establish the idea of extinction as a fact through his comparison of fossil bones with those of existing animals. Through his work, and that of many other paleontologists, it was shown that, in the past, the world had been populated with countless species, most of which had gone extinct over the course of hundreds of millions of years. While some species faded away over many millennia, there also seem to have been "extinction events," when tremendous numbers of species went extinct in a relatively short (geologically speaking) period of time. The most recent of these is the Holocene extinction, which began about 12,000 years ago and is still in progress.

In North America, the Holocene Extinction Event was particularly extreme, as the continent lost over 70% of its megafauna, those animal species which exceed 44 kilograms in weight. Thirty-seven genera of mammals disappeared completely. These included mastodons, mammoths, giant ground sloths, giant armadillos, camels, dire wolves, saber-toothed cats, cave bears, horses, and numerous other animals that had thrived on the continent prior to this time.

Once it was accepted that many members of the megafauna actually had gone extinct, folks immediately began theorizing about what led to the total demise of such large and wide-spread creatures. Since it became increasingly obvious, particularly in the Americas, that the extinction of key species was closely correlated in time with colonization by humans, extinction as a result of hunting by *Homo sapiens* became a popular explanation for the phenomena. Additional evidence was provided by a number of archaeological discoveries of ancient camp sites and "kill sites" where the bones of extinct animals were found intermixed with human stone weapons, butchering tools and cooking hearths.

The latest theories regarding the Holocene Extinction postulate that, in addition to human action, changes in the climate also played a major role in the dramatic changes in animal communities. According to these, as the environment warmed and the glaciers receded at the end of the last Ice Age, habitats for large species became increasingly fragmented, creating increasing stress on the megafauna, so that the appearance of human hunters was the final blow for already weakened populations.

The latest extinction event is still continuing. In the Americas, something of an equilibrium was achieved lasting for thousands of years between the initial human invasion thousands of years ago, and the subsequent arrival of a new wave of humans from Europe and elsewhere, beginning around 1500 AD. The newcomers, with their vastly improved hunting technology and their relentless conversion of native habitat to farm land, came very close to eliminating such megafauna as remained in North America. Large predators, the cougars, bears, and wolves were among the first to go, followed by large Eastern Woodland herbivores, deer and moose. As human expansion moved westward, the vast herds of millions of bison were virtually wiped out, as were species of antelope, wild sheep and mountain goats. By 1950, four species of wolf, the eastern cougar, two species of elk, and two of bear had been hunted into extinction. Other species, such as bison, remained only as tiny, scattered fragments rapidly declining into oblivion.

The "environmental movement," which has experienced tremendous growth since the 1960s, has reversed, at least temporarily, the decline of many of the larger, most obvious species – the remaining megafauna – even as numerous less noticeable, or "less desirable," species of animals and plants continue to vanished from the earth. More recently, however, the effects of climate change, coupled with increased environmental destruction for agricultural purposes, mineral extraction, and industrial and residential development are threatening to destroy much of the progress that has been made.

Mammoths and Mastodons

Mammoths and Mastodons were among the largest mammals that disappeared from North America towards the end of the Pleistocene Age, around 10,000 to 12,000 years ago. Mastodons were similar in appearance to modern day elephants, to which were only distantly related. They lived in herds and were vegetarians who browsed and grazed, primarily in wooded areas. Individuals measured around eight or nine feet tall at the shoulder and weighed between eight and twelve tons.

Mammoths, sometimes known as wooly mammoths because they were covered with dense fur, were much more closely related to our elephants, and were somewhat larger than mastodons with fatty humps on their backs to store nutrients. They were a more northern species adapted to living on frozen tundras and grazing on low vegetation. The bones and mummified bodies of mammoths are frequently found in areas where the permafrost is melting due to increasing global temperatures.

Humans, both *Homo sapiens* and some of our early ancestors ate elephant meat over the course of hundreds of thousands of years. Evidence of such a feast held by Heidleberg man, *Homo heidelbergensis*, turned up in Kent, England, where a 400,000 year old skeleton of an extinct species of elephant was found along with the flint tools that they used to butcher it.

There is abundant evidence that humans, hunted and ate the mammoth in North America. Camp sites with bones of the great beasts intermixed with stone cutting tools have been found and even the remains of carcasses with spear points still embedded in the bones and marks of butchering clearly visible. The Clovis people, a rather mysterious group of proto-Indians, appear to have avidly pursued the great mammoths, killing them with spears tipped with remarkably beautiful and well-crafted stone points.

For many years it was an accepted fact that over-hunting of mammoth and other members of the megafauna was the primary cause of their extinction. Recently, however, it has become clearer that it was due more to a combination of factors, with humans adding the final, fatal blow to populations that were strained and weakened by environmental changes associated with the ending of the most recent Ice Age.

RECIPES:

We can assume that Paleolithic hunters were not conversant with complicated methods of food preparation. Roasting over open fires, in earth ovens, or in coatings of clay would have been the most common techniques. Prior to the invention of pottery, extended boiling would not have been possible. Some idea of the method of preparation of mammoth and mastodon can be gained from the accounts of dining on elephant written by folks who experienced it in relatively recent times.

Dr. David Livingstone, of "I presume" fame, described dining on elephant in his 1864 journal. Elephant foot was a popular item, perhaps because it was one on the more easily removed transported portions of the beast. It was generally cooked underground in an earth oven.

"We had the foot thus cooked for breakfast next morning, and found it delicious. It is a whitish mass, slightly gelatinous, and sweet, like marrow. A long march, to prevent biliousness, is a wise precaution after a meal of elephant's foot. Elephant's trunk and tongue are also good, and, after long simmering, much resemble the hump of a buffalo, and the tongue of an ox; but all the other meat is tough, and, from its peculiar flavour, only to be eaten by a hungry man."

A recipe for preparing elephant foot was given in more detail by Sir Samuel Baker in 1868.

A hole should be dug in the earth, about four feet deep, and two feet six inches in diameter...in this a large fire should be lighted, and kept burning for four or five hours...so that the walls become red-hot. At the expiration of the blaze, the foot should be laid upon the glowing embers, and the hole covered closely with thick pieces of green wood...to form a ceiling; this should be covered with wet grass, and the whole plastered with mud, and stamped tightly down to retain the heat. [T]he oven should not be opened for thirty hours, or more. At the expiration of that time, the foot will be perfectly baked, and the sole will separate like a shoe, and expose a delicate substance that, with a little oil and vinegar, together with an allowance of pepper and salt, is a delicious dish that will feed about fifty men.

Leipoldt, in his *Cape Cookery,* is less enthusiastic. "The foot, baked in an improvised oven or under the ashes, is regarded by many as a delicacy, but actually has little to commend it."

CONSERVATION STATUS: EXTINCT

Given the large number of moderately well-preserved frozen carcasses of mammoths that have been salvaged from the melting permafrost recently, the prospect of recreating the mammoth from sequenced DNA using modern day elephants as surrogate mothers is quite good. Work on this project is already underway in several laboratories.

3. MAMMAL COOKERY

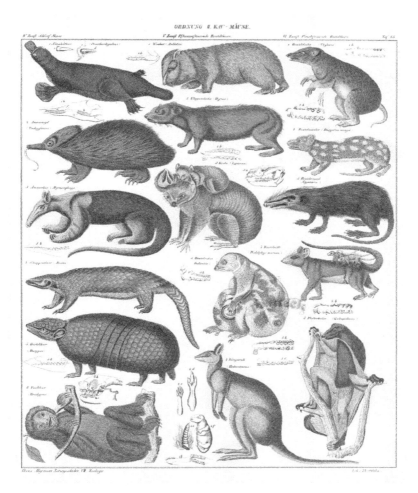

No one knows for certain how many species of organisms there are currently living on Earth. Estimates vary from 2 million to 2 billion and even, according to one recent calculation, as many as a trillion. Of these, around 6,000 species are mammals, of which a mere handful are commonly used as food by humans. Pigs and cattle head the list, followed distantly by sheep, goats and buffalo. Many of the other mammals are consumed, at least occasionally, by humans, even a number of very prominent species that are well known to be on the very edge of extinction. Human hunger and greed are both powerful motivators against which even the strongest and most resourceful animals stand little chance.

We may never know how many species of mammals have gone extinct through direct or indirect human action. Many we have obviously eaten into oblivion, while many others were simply destroyed by accident or slaughtered as pests.

Although the extinction of mammalian megafauna has traditionally received the most attention, a vast number of smaller species are currently endangered or have passed into oblivion, many without ever having ever been observed or named by humans. A great many species, particularly those on isolated islands, were wiped out by non-native predators, often domestic cats and more European rats, escaped from the ships of early explorers. Despite out much greater knowledge and environmental awareness, the destruction still goes on, as humans continue to consume some of our most endangered mammals and relentlessly destroy the habitats of innumerable others, known or now and forever unknown.

Pangolin

Until recently, few people had ever heard of the pangolin yet, now at the time of this writing, they are the most commonly illegally captured and trafficked wild animal in the world. This is another case where human greed, coupled with human stupidity, seem likely to drive a perfectly harmless animal to the brink of extinction, and quite possibly over it.

There are eight species of pangolin, which range in size from 12 to 39 inches. They are the only mammals to be covered in scales, made of keratin, which gives them an appearance somewhere between a pine cone and a reptile. When frightened, they can curl into an armored ball which provides excellent protection against predators. They generally are nocturnal, solitary and secretive, living in holes in the ground or hollows in trees, and feed primarily on ants and termites. All pangolin species are endangered, some critically so.

This inoffensive and environmentally important animal – it is crucial to the control of termites in many areas – appears doomed because of a conjunction of destructive factors. It apparently is quite tasty, making it a favorite form of "bush meat." It's habitat is rapidly disappearing, being cleared for cultivation of crops. It generally produces only one offspring a year, making replacement of depleted populations slow and difficult. It is rather delicate in terms of health and has a very specialized diet, making it very hard to maintain in zoos or breeding facilities, with most captured individuals dying very quickly. And to cap it all off, pangolin are highly sought after both for gourmet meals and for that most pernicious and unnecessary purpose, traditional Chinese medicine, which uses tens of thousands of them annually. Pangolin scales, blood, and even unborn fetuses are used to treat a whole range of conditions, despite there being no scientific proof that they are in any way effective.

The most recent surveys have estimated that in Africa alone between 400,000 and 2,700,000 pangolin are killed each year.

RECIPE:

Although a great number of pangolin are said to be eaten throughout Asia and Africa, recipes for cooking them seem to be unavailable, at least in English. Many of them are consumed as bush meat in areas where they are found and commonly are roasted over open fires, boiled, or cut up and used in a variety of dishes. The scales are always saved, since they bring very high prices when sold for medical uses. They are also used in gourmet "status dishes" served in exclusive restaurants in China and elsewhere.

CONSERVATION STATUS: CRITICALLY ENDANGERED

The World Wildlife Fund and other organizations are working to reduce both poaching of pangolin and the demand for products made from them in the traditional medicine markets. The species has been protected globally since 2016 under the Convention on International Trade in Endangered Species of Wild Fauna and Flora (CITES). Unfortunately, the illegal trade in pangolin and pangolin body parts, particularly their scales, still continues on a fairly large scale and their local consumption as bush meat is almost impossible to control. Given their widespread distribution and their secretive nature, it is likely that some members of one or more species will survive in remote areas, as long as any such areas remain on earth.

Giraffe

Prêtre pinx!   *Turpin direx!*   *M.r Massard sculp!*

LA GIRAFE.

Despite the fact that giraffes can be seen in virtually every zoo of any size, they are, in actuality, becoming increasingly threatened in the wild, with population size estimated in 2018 to be between 80,000 and 111,000 individuals, down from

155,000 in the 1980s. The giraffe is found only in Africa, in nine geographically separated populations, traditionally considered subspecies, all of which are considered vulnerable, with two being listed as critically endangered. Part of the decline is due to continuing habitat destruction, but the greater portion is the result of hunting by humans. There are always chronic meat shortages for poorer folks in much of Africa and a giraffe represents several hundred pounds of it in an easy to find and relatively easy to kill form. Compared to some other large animals, little research has been done on giraffe conservation, but if current trends continue both in poaching for food, and to a more limited extent, trophy hunting, it is possible that the giraffe will be extinct in the wild in a matter of decades.

RECIPES:

As with much "bush meat," formal recipes for cooking giraffe are hard to come by. The following is from Leipoldt's *Cape Cookery.*

Giraffe meat is coarse and stringy, but parts of it are excellent, and the long, succulent tongue, properly cooked is not only eatable but delectable. The expectant cook will be much disappointed to learn that the animal's well-developed bones are quite useless for marrow bones; with every care, all that results when such a bone is boiled or baked, is a mess of yellow, unappetizing oil that cannot be coaxed to a consistency that will enable it to adjust itself to a piece of toast.

Usually, large wild herbivores are cooked like beef or venison, often grilled over open fires. In 1991, a giraffe barbeque was held in South Africa in which 16 gallons of sauce were used to marinate a carcass weighing in at 1,880 pounds.

The meat was roasted on a twenty foot long custom made spit and served to about 1,000 paying guests.

CONSERVATION STATUS: Vulnerable to extinction, with some populations critically endangered.

Given that giraffes are popular attractions in zoos and wildlife preserves, and that they breed reasonably well in captivity, it is unlikely that they will go completely extinct. However, it is probable that some of the population groups, be they species or subspecies, will not survive in the wild or captivity. The open savannahs and woodlands they inhabit are quite vulnerable both to the effects of climate change and development and offer no real areas of concealment to such a large species. Giraffes are still hunted illegally for bush meat and, in some areas, legally by trophy hunters who pay large fees for the privilege.

Bulmer's Fruit Bat *Aproteles bulmerae*

Fliegender Hund (Pteropus edulis). ¼

Fruit bat similar to Bulmer's

There are approximately 1,200 bat species worldwide, representing about 20% of known mammals. Of these, 24 species are listed as critically endangered, 53 endangered, and 104 vulnerable.   In actuality, virtually all bat species are vulnerable to habitat loss, disease, human hunting, loss of food species, wind generators, and other threats. In North America, the fungal disease, White Nose Syndrome , has killed millions of bats and is considered one of the worst wildlife diseases in modern times.

Bats range in size from the smallest known mammal, a hog-nosed bat weighing less than a tenth of an ounce, to flying foxes, fruit eating bats that can weigh over 2 pounds. One of the flying foxes, Bulmer's Fruit Bat, is probably the most endangered bat on the planet.

Bulmer's Fruit Bat is a cave dwelling species that, although long known to locals, was only discovered by science in 1975 in a single cave, known as Luplupwintem, in Western Province, Papua New Guinea. At that time there were thousands of the bats and, probably due to the difficulty of reaching them in the cave, the locals consumed them at a rate which allowed the population to maintain themselves at a sustainable level. However, after the existence of the tasty bats was brought to the attention of outsiders with ropes and shotguns, who hunted for the "bush meat" market and blasted bats off the walls with shotguns, the population was reduced to near the point of extinction within two years. Indeed, it was believed that the species was extinct until 1993, when a colony of 160 of the bats was discovered in the same cave. Populations of Bulmer's fruit bats were known to have occurred in at least two other locations, but the status of these is unknown. The species is currently listed as Critically Endangered.

RECIPE:

Flying fox with prunes and cream sauce [After a New Caledonian Recipe, R. J. May 1984]

6 flying foxes	Flour
500g prunes	50g butter
300ml white wine	1 tbsp red currant jelly
Salt, pepper	200 ml thick cream

Remove the flesh from the flying foxes. To do this, either plunge the animals in boiling water for a while then skin them and remove the flesh from the bones, or roast the animals for a little while on an open fire, remove and when cool, break open down the backbone and remove the flesh from the skin.

Soak the prunes overnight in 250ml of the wine (a little more if the prunes are very dry). Before using, gently heat the prunes in the wine for about 10 minutes.

Season the flying fox meat with salt and pepper and roll in flour. Heat the butter and cook the meat on low heat until brown. Add the rest of the wine, cover and cook for a further 20 minutes. Next add the juice from the prunes. Transfer the prunes themselves to a serving dish and keep warm in a low oven.

After the meat has cooked another 10 minutes or so, and the juice reduced a little, remove the meat and place on the serving dish with the prunes. To the sauce in the pan, now add the red currant jelly (cranberry sauce is not a bad substitute) and mix thoroughly. Then, a little at a time, add the cream to form a thick, smooth sauce.

Pour this over the flying fox and prunes and serve.

CONSERVATION STATUS: CRITICALLY ENDANGERED

Bulmer's Fruit Bat is unlikely to survive due to its small population size, slow rate of reproduction, exploitation for bush meat, and increasing human intrusion into its habitat. It is considered to be a priority species for conservation, but due to its remote location, both monitoring and protecting the species are extremely difficult.

Rhinoceros

The five existing species of rhinoceros are the last of a great number of different types of rhinos that roamed much of the earth from about 40 million years ago until the present day. The Sumatran rhinoceros is said to be the oldest species of mammal living today. It is critically endangered. As of this writing, fewer than 80 individuals remain in the wild. It is quite possible that, by the time you read this, the species will have become extinct. The Javan rhino, with fewer than 70 living individuals is also in imminent danger of extinction.

All rhinoceros living in the wild are in danger of being slaughtered by poachers, who kill them for their horns, which can be worth more than gold on the black market. The horns, which are made of keratin, like hair and fingernails, are another example of a totally ineffective substance being sold on the black market as a "traditional" medicine. The incredible prices being paid for the worthless substance almost guarantee the extermination of rhinos in the wild.

RECIPE:

As noted, rhinos are killed primarily for their horns, and remainder of the carcass is often left behind to rot by the poachers, so few descriptions of rhinoceros cookery are available. The Rev. John Campbell who traveled in South Africa in 1822, described the following method for cooking choice bits of the giant beasts.

In order to cook the lower legs and hoofs of the rhinoceros, an ant's nest is selected, being a structure of hard clay about three feet high, and shaped like a bee-hive; the inside is a cellular turfy substance, which being removed and the cavity heated by burning brushwood, within it an excellent oven is prepared for the purpose.

CONSERVATION STATUS: 3 species CRITICALLY
ENDANGERED. 1 species NEAR THREATENED.
1 species VULNERABLE.

The outlook is cautiously optimistic for Black Rhinos, Greater One-horned Rhinos, and White Rhinos, all of whose populations have been increasing in the wild due to extraordinary protection efforts in wildlife reserves and zoological parks. Survival is very uncertain for Javan and Sumatran rhinos, due to very low population numbers and quite small habitat sizes.

The Great Whales

Fig. 194.—Whale-Fishing.—Fac-simile of a Woodcut in the "Cosmographie Universelle" of Thevet, in folio: Paris, 1574.

Whale fishing, for food and oil, has probably gone on in one form or another whenever or wherever humans lived close to the sea. Until the great age of sail, however, it was usually conducted from, or very close to shore, as whales appeared in the vicinity, and had very little impact on cetacean populations. The rather unusual specimen [note the breasts] in the woodcut above, appears to have been snagged with an anchor and hauled ashore with ropes. The capture of such a bounty of food was obviously a cause for celebration with bagpipes and banners.

During the height of the whale fishery [under sail], the main products sought were oil for lamps and lubrication and whalebone, properly known as baleen, the thin parallel plates of elastic keratin used by some varieties of whales to strain plankton from the seawater. Whalebone, when heated and bent, would retain the shape when cooled and was very useful for stays in corsets, ribs of umbrellas, hoops for skirts, buggy whips, and a number of other items generally made of plastic today.

When we think of whaling, we tend to envision the days of Moby Dick, with sailing ships, men in open whaleboats, and hand thrown harpoons. Sailing ships are estimated to have taken about 300,000 sperm whales between 1700 and the 1890s. In reality, the greatest slaughter of whales took place in the days of motorized ships with guns launching explosive harpoons and, most recently, huge "factory ships." It is estimated that between 1900 and 1999, almost three million whales were slaughtered by commercial operations. Whale products were used in many industries, including cosmetics, lubricants, insecticides, candles, pet food, and fertilizer. NASA even utilized spermaceti as a lubricant in the space program.

In the United States, eating whale meat never caught on. In 1918, in response to food shortages resulting from World War I, the Department of Commerce's Bureau of Fisheries attempted to convince American housewives to put whale meat on the family dining table. Their efforts produced a cookbook entitled, *Whales and Porpoises as Food, with Thirty-two Recipes.* Many of these recipes sound extraordinarily bizarre, for example, stuffed roast whale, whale patty, or,

RECIPES

WHALE CROQUETTES

3 cups cold roast whale meat.
2 sprigs parsley.
1 large onion
2 teaspoons salt.

Pepper.

3 tablespoons melted butter

1 teaspoon savory (optional).

6-8 walnut meats (optional).

Chop and mix the meat, parsley, and onion; add the salt, pepper, butter, savory and nut meats. Moisten with just sufficient gravyto hold the mixture together. Shape into croquettes, roll in bread crumbs, dip in slightly beaten egg to which a tablespoon of cold water has been added, roll again in crumbs and fry in deep fat for about 8 minutes. Garnish with parsley and sweet pickles and serve at once.

Canned whale meat, as well as the fresh product, was also touted by the Bureau of fisheries.

WHALE MEAT PIE

Worcestershire Sauce

Salt

Pepper

1 pound canned whale meat

3 onions

3 tablespoons butter

½ pound bacon

Cut the meat into small pieces. Slice onions and put in a frying pan with butter and cook slowly until browned. Cut the bacon into small pieces and fry for a few minutes. Drain and moisten with Worcestershire Sauce. Mix all with the canned whale meat, season to taste and put into a deep dish which has been lined with pie crust, moistening the edges of the dish so that the pie crust will adhere. Cut some pie crust the size of the dish and place on top. Brush the top with a beaten egg, cook in oven until well browned, and serve. It may be made into individual pies.

CONSERVATION STATUS: CRITICALLY ENDANGERED to LEAST CONCERN.

Varies by species and by populations within species. Blue whale populations range from Endangered to Critically Endangered; Gray whales from Least Concern to Critically Endangered; Fin whales are Endangered; Right whales from Threatened to Endangered; Sei whales are Endangered; Sperm whales are Vulnerable, Bowhead whales are Threatened; Beluga are Near Threatened. The Southern bottlenose whale, Bowhead whale, Humpback whale, and Melon-headed whale are listed as being of Least Concern.

The prognosis for survival is "cautiously optimistic." In general whale populations have increased significantly since the appearance of the "Save the Whales" campaign in the 1960s and the moratorium on most commercial whaling enacted by the International Whaling Commission in 1986. The recent resumption of commercial whaling by the Japanese, however, is seen as a possible indicator of a return to large scale whaling in the near future. A potentially much greater danger to whale populations has become apparent very recently in the form of the tremendous volume of plastic waste that it is flooding the oceans of the world.

An increasing number of whales of a variety of species are being found dead with large volumes of plastic in their stomachs. Some have starved to death because they could not take sufficient food into their plastic stuffed bellies and others have had their internal organs pierced by sharp edges on the waste they have consumed. Whales also die as a result of becoming entangled in plastic fishing gear, ropes and nets, both discarded and in active use.

In addition to plastics, other forms of pollution, along with the decreasing numbers of prey species, the effects of climate change, and the increasing numbers of collisions with large vessels all place at risk the continuing recovery of the great whales.

Prairie Dogs

Prairie dogs are a type of burrowing ground squirrel, historically found primarily in the vast grassland prairies west of the Mississippi River. They are considered to be a "keystone species," one which is critical to the health of the local ecosystem. Once they numbered in the hundreds of millions, living in "towns" of underground burrows ranging in area from perhaps half a square mile to the largest recorded one which covered 25,000 square miles in Texas and was occupied by several hundred million prairie dogs.

The importance of the species in the ecosystem was primarily as a readily available source of food for numerous predators, including foxes, ferrets, coyotes, badgers, and hawks. For many of these they represent the primary prey species, without which survival might be impossible. Prairie dogs also provide homes for a number of other species in their burrows, including other ground squirrels, plover and burrowing owls.

Since the Great Plains were settled and largely converted to farming and grazing, prairie dogs have been fanatically destroyed, largely by poisoning, reducing their numbers to perhaps 2% of the original population, scattered throughout 5% of their former range. The various other species which were dependent upon them suffered comparable reductions in their numbers.

In addition to persecution by humans and habitat loss, the species is also extremely susceptible to bubonic plague which can destroy the populations of entire towns.

There are five species of prairie dog, all of which have been dramatically reduced in numbers. Of these, the Mexican and Utah prairie dogs are endangered. Utah prairie dogs currently number less than 5,000.

RECIPES:

GRILLED PRAIRIE DOG (Navajo Recipe)

5 Fresh prairie dogs (caught in early spring)
Onions
Pepper
Salt
Garlic

Clean and quarter prairie dogs, pat dry. Add onions, pepper, salt and garlic. Place on grill and cook slowly for about ½ hour. Be careful not to overcook.

CONSERVATION STATUS: THREATENED: Utah and Mexican prairie dogs. Black-tailed, White-tailed and Gunnison's prairie dogs: numbers declining but not listed as threatened or endangered.

In addition to persecution by humans, habitat destruction, effects of climate change and bubonic plague, the recent conservation success in restoring populations of the near extinct black-footed ferret has also been taking an increasing toll on prairie dogs. The ferret feeds almost exclusively on prairie dogs and can devastate populations already weakened by other factors.

Gorillas

There are two existing species of gorilla, the Western gorilla, *Gorilla gorilla*, with two subspecies, the Western Lowland gorilla and Cross River gorilla, and the Eastern gorilla, *Gorilla*

berengei, with subspecies Mountain gorilla and Eastern Lowland gorilla. All are listed as critically endangered.

It is extremely difficult to determine the population size of these "great apes" since the majority live in some of the most remote and impenetrable regions of Equatorial Africa, a number of which are also areas of armed conflict. According to recent estimations, which must be considered as very approximate and subject to rapid change, there are:

Western Lowland gorilla. Approximately 100,000, of which 550 are in zoos.
Eastern Lowland gorilla. 3,800 with one female in captivity
Mountain gorilla. 880
Cross River gorilla. 250

All of the gorilla species are steadily declining in number, with the primary causes being humans hunting them for "bushmeat" and the pet trade, habitat destruction by logging and mineral extraction operations, and most troubling, by disease. Recent outbreaks of Ebola have devastated populations of the Western Lowland species, killing up to 95% of affected groups. It was the terrible effects of the Ebola virus that caused the relatively numerous Western gorillas to be moved from the endangered category to critically endangered.

Logging, mining and hunting for bushmeat go hand in hand as new roads cut to harvest the resources allow hunters to move deeper into what previously were nearly impenetrable gorilla forest and swamp habitat. Bushmeat hunting often is highly organized, carried out by specialist hunters who either directly, or more commonly through a chain of middlemen, supply gorilla meat and the flesh of other endangered animals to high-end gourmet restaurants in some of the large cities in Africa.

The loss of gorilla populations can prove devastating to entire ecosystems. The large mammals play a key role as seed dispersers. Gorillas eat a wide variety of fruits and excrete most seeds in a still viable state in their feces, both at their nesting sites and as they move browsing through the forests. By moving the seeds from their point of origin to other locations they assist in creating and maintaining a healthy mix of plant species throughout their environment.

RECIPIES

Although eating the flesh of our close relatives is repugnant to many, for some, both the starving local people and wealthy gourmets seeking the unusual, gorilla meat makes a highly desirable meal. The flesh is generally described as being rather like rich, smoky veal. The hands and feet are said to be the most favored parts.

Gorilla Stew (traditional recipe)

Ingredients:

1 gorilla
Water
Oil
Vegetables as available
Spices including wild pepper, salt
Herbs including cassava leaves, cocoyam leaves

Butcher gorilla into pieces, singe off the hair.

In a large pot boil body parts, excluding head, with water, oil salt and spices, herbs and vegetables for two hours.

Put the entire head, including brain and eyes, in its own pot of boiling water and oil, cook until the flesh falls off, then add flesh to the stew.

Retain skull for magical purposes, if desired.

CONSERVATION STATUS: CRITICALLY ENDANGERED

The continual decline of all varieties of gorilla is probable. Female gorillas generally don't begin to breed until about 10 years of age and then only produce offspring every four to six years, making it extremely slow and difficult to increase the size of depleted populations. It is possible that two of the subspecies, the Mountain and Cross River Gorillas will go extinct in the near future. The Western Lowland Gorilla, with a population near 100,000 individuals, and with a substantial number kept in zoos, will likely continue to exist in the wild – as long as wild and remote areas continue to exist and remain relatively free of armed human conflicts.

4. BIRDS

Since 1500 AD, somewhere between 150 and 190 species of birds, that we know of, have become extinct, and data indicates that the pace of bird extinction has been accelerating. Of the approximately 11,000 known species of birds on Earth, as of 2018, 1,469 were in danger of extinction. The usual culprits, hunting and habitat destruction are largely responsible, with the majority of bird extinctions occurring on isolated islands, mostly in the Pacific. The Hawaiian Islands are considered the bird extinction capital of the world, with two thirds of its unique bird species having become extinct since the first humans arrived.

Passenger pigeon

The disappearance of the Passenger Pigeon in the early 1900s, must surely have convinced even the most skeptical individuals that entire species really could cease to exist. This bird, which was quite similar to a larger and more colorful mourning dove, was found only on the North American

Continent, primarily in the great forest that originally stretched almost unbroken from the Atlantic Coast to the Mississippi River. It has been estimated that at the start of the European invasion of the Americas the population of passenger pigeons numbered somewhere between 3 and 5 billion birds. Their migratory flocks were said to darken the sky for days as they passed and that the weight of roosting birds would break branches and sometimes fell entire trees.

On Tuesday, September 1, 1914, the last surviving member of the species, a 29 year old bird named Martha, pictured above, died in a cage at the Cincinnati Zoo. The passenger pigeon, which might have been the most numerous avian species on earth for tens of thousands of years, was totally wiped out by human actions during a very brief period, primarily between 1850 and 1910.

As was often the case, several human related causes combined to drive the species to extinction. The pigeons had always been hunted by the folks who lived under their migration route, but the number that could be consumed locally barely made a dent in the immense population. However, the advent of the railroads made it possible to rapidly ship boxcar loads of the birds to the restaurants in New York, Boston and other large cities. In addition to this, the increasing popularity of cookbooks, many featuring recipes for passenger pigeon, also increased the demand for the inexpensive and tasty birds.

It is possible that the passenger pigeon might have survived all of this, though in greatly reduced numbers, if it were not for clearing of the vast eastern forests that they required for nesting, roosting, and for the acorns and other vegetation on which they fed. As agriculture expanded, the passenger pigeons declined in number until finally the social structure that this communally nesting species required collapsed, and with the passing of the last captive birds, the species ceased to exist.

RECIPE:

PASSENGER PIGEON PIE [S.T. Rorer, 1886]

Pick and clean four wild pigeons, the same as chicken. Cut them into halves, put them into a baking-pan, baste with melted butter, and bake in a quick oven for forty-five minutes, basting with melted butter, salt and pepper every ten minutes, using in all about two tablespoonfuls of butter, a half-teaspoon of salt, and a dash of pepper. At the end of this time, take them out.

Line a two-quart tin basin or a raised pie-mould with plain butter paste. Have ready one pound of ham cut into dice, six hard-boiled eggs sliced. Put a layer of pigeons in the bottom, then ham, then eggs, then salt, pepper, and a few bits of butter, then pigeon, and so on, until all is used. Cover with a thick sheet of paste; make a hole in the center, and ornament with some leaves and flowers cut out of the paste trimmings. Bake in a quick oven for thirty minutes, or until the paste is done.

Put two tablespoonfuls of butter in the pan in which they were roasted, stir it over the fire until a nice brown, then add two tablespoonfuls of flour, and mix until smooth; add one pint of boiling water, salt and pepper to taste; stir continually until it boils; take from fire, add the beaten yolk of one egg, and pour into the pie through a funnel, placed in the hole in the center of top crust, and it is ready to serve. It is most delicious.

Tame pigeons may be used, but are not as good as the wild ones.

Blackbird pie may be made the same as Pigeon Pie, using one dozen blackbirds instead of four pigeons.

CONSERVATION STATUS: EXTINCT

Experiments are in progress to de-extinct the passenger pigeon using gene editing techniques. While these might possibly produce a bird similar to the extinct one, it is unlikely that they could succeed in bringing back a species that could not be kept successfully in captivity and which required huge flocks to survive in the wild.

Flamingo

From the evidence of nature videos, which show vast flocks of shocking pink flamingos feeding in shallow waters, you might reasonably believe that the birds are not endangered, and technically most of the several species are not.   The problem is that they generally breed and feed in some of the most hostile habitats on earth, many of which are quite vulnerable to serious habitat degradation or elimination through the effects of climate change.

Although flamingos are found in a wide variety of areas and climatic zones throughout the world, they are wading birds which, in order to feed, require water with a high salt concentration that is neither too deep nor too shallow in alkaline lakes and lagoons with muddy bottoms, little vegetation and few if any fish to compete with them for food. The birds filter-feed on brine shrimp, algae, and other small aquatic life-forms, using their specialized bills to separate food from the mud and silt while wading and sometimes swimming if the water is too deep.

Although flamingo populations as a whole are in no immediate danger, in recent years a number of local populations have gone extinct or been greatly reduced in numbers due to agricultural and industrial pollution and desertification.

RECIPES:

C. Louis Leipoldt, in his *Cape Cookery,* notes that flamingo flesh is

Perhaps the most tender, tasty and delicately flavored, possibly because the bird feeds on an aquatic plankton diet that imparts to its meat an extraordinary savory quality...When grilled, it is practically indistinguishable from beef as far as color is concerned, but its tenderness is far superior and it seldom needs larding.

He also provides the following recipe.

STUFFED BREAST OF FLAMINGO

Carefully remove the flesh from both sides of the breastbone and place it in red wine for a couple of hours; wipe dry and rub pepper and salt and a little pounded chilli. Take a fairly coherent farce [a stuffing, usually of ground meat]; mould it to fit inside of the two breast pieces; wrap them round the farce and skewer with wooden pegs or bind with string. Put in a saucepan with a few cups of red wine, a bit of lemon peel or scented verbena, a few cloves and a handful of small onions. Let it simmer gently till tender; thicken the gravy with a white sauce and serve.

CONSERVATION STATUS: UNCERTAIN

Breeding populations are maintained in captivity, but dramatic climate shifts and increased industrial and agricultural development in Africa and elsewhere could result in dramatic population reductions in the wild.

Nene, the Hawaiian Goose

It has often been said that the Hawaiian Islands are the extinction capitol of the world. Since the start of the European invasion in 1778 a vast number of indigenous species that were found nowhere else in the world have been driven to extinction through direct human activities as well as the introduction of "exotic" predators and new competitors for limited food resources. A partial list of species that have become extinct since "first contact" includes 28 species of bird, 72 snails, 74 insects, and 97 plants. A number of the remaining species are struggling for survival, but a few are actually increasing in number due to the heroic efforts of government agencies, non-profit organizations, zoologists and an army of dedicated volunteers. One species that has been brought back from the very edge of extinction, to the point where it is currently being reintroduced into the wild, is the 'alala, the Hawaiian crow. Even more successful has been the rescue of the Nene, the Hawaiian Goose.

The nene is a close relative of the Canada goose whose ancestors arrived soon after the formation of the volcanic Hawaiian Islands, 890,000 years or so ago. It is estimated that there were around 25,000 nene on the various islands in 1778. By 1952 the population had been reduced to just 30 birds, through a combination of hunting and depredation by a number of introduced predators. Fortunately, geese breed well in captivity, and the few remaining birds were removed to nature reserves and ultimately reintroduced to the wild. Currently there are in the neighborhood of 2,500 nene on the islands and in a number of zoos and conservation centers.

RECIPES:

In all probability, nene was cooked by roasting or boiling in past times. The following is not an authentic recipe, simply a method of cooking goose "Hawaiian style."

SLOW COOKED HAWAIIAN GOOSE.

Ingredients

> 4 goose breasts
> buttermilk to cover goose breasts, 1-2 cups
> 2 bottles barbecue sauce
> 1 can pineapple tidbits + ½ the juice
> 1 green pepper, sliced
> 1 onion, chopped
> 4 garlic cloves, minced

Instructions

1. Soak goose for 6-8 hours in salt water then drain. Rinse then cover the goose with plain water overnight. Drain and cover with buttermilk. Soak for at least 3 hours.
2. Slice the goose breasts.
3. Combine all the other ingredients together in a bowl to make the sauce.
4. Layer ingredients in the slow cooker starting with a thin layer of sauce. Alternate half the goose and half the sauce, ending with the sauce.
5. Cook on low for 8-9 hours.
6. Serve over rice.

CONSERVATION STATUS: VULNERABLE

Given the number of nene kept in many different locations, it seems extremely unlikely that any event could destroy the entire population. There is some concern over the small size of the gene pool that could result in genetic defects.

Greater Prairie Chicken

The fate of the Greater Prairie Chicken or pinnated grouse, *Tympanuchus cupido*, of America's Midwest, rivals that of the much better known passenger pigeon. Before the plow arrived, the tall grass prairies that covered much of the middle of the North American continent, were home to many millions of prairie chicken. Unlike the passenger pigeon, they were not social birds traveling in gigantic, impossible to miss, flocks, but more solitary animals, with individual territories spaced out over hundreds of thousands of square miles.

The greater prairie chicken is a ground nesting species and, as such, is subject to a wide range of natural dangers, many of which have been made worse by climate change. Floods can destroy nests and drown chicks and drought can eliminate the food the young depend on. A variety of predators including snakes, foxes, raptors, raccoons, opossums and coyotes, among others, feed eggs, young and adults.

The real threats to the prairie chickens were the same two that drove the passenger pigeon into extinction, habitat conversion for agricultural use and intense hunting by humans both for sport and the pot. Like the pigeon, millions of prairie chickens are said to have been killed and shipped via railroad to the markets and restaurants in New York, Chicago and other big cities.

These combined pressures drove the species close to extinction by the 1930s. Areas that previously served as habitat for millions of the birds have seen them extirpated or reduced to small remnant populations. In Canada, Alberta, Saskatchewan, Manitoba, and Ontario have seen their entire populations wiped out. Illinois recorded only 200 greater prairie chickens in 2019. Iowa, Missouri, and Wisconsin each are home to less than a thousand.

Despite the fact that the species has been extirpated from much of its former range, fairly large populations still exist in Kansas, Nebraska, and the Dakotas, numbering perhaps 400,000 – 500,000 birds. These populations, however, are also in decline.

RECIPE:

The Home Comfort Range Company made a number of very popular wood stoves for many years. They also published a cookbook around 1900 for those using their product. This included the following recipe for prairie chicken.

Ingredients

Prairie chicken
Salt
Pepper
Butter

After preparing, boil in hot water until quite tender in all the joints except the breast; take out and rub all over with butter; salt, and pepper, and boil briskly with the breast; then take out again and with a lump of butter on each piece set in the oven for a very short time.

In general, any recipe for chicken can be used, however, the flesh of the prairie chicken will be much darker with a richer flavor.

CONSERVATION STATUS: THREATENED

Despite its "threatened" status, the greater prairie chicken is still legally hunted in several states. It is probable that populations will continue to decline, though a number of protected refuges have been established, so total extinction is unlikely in the near future.

Great Auk

Despite its appearance and its scientific name, *Pinguinus impennis,* the now extinct great auk was not a penguin. Unlike penguins, which live almost exclusively in the southern hemisphere, the great auk lived in the cold coastal regions of the Atlantic Ocean from Canada across to northern Europe. As its name implies, it was a large bird, standing 30 to 33 inches tall and weighed about 11 pounds. It was very familiar to seafarers and folks living along the Atlantic coasts and when explorers encountered birds with a similar appearance in the southern hemisphere they gave them its Latin name, despite the fact that the birds were only distantly related.

The great auk had the disadvantage of spending most of its life at sea and utilizing rocky, isolated islands for breeding purposes. A plentiful food supply was necessary for the huge flocks that gathered in breeding season, which meant that there were not a great number of locations that met all their requirements. Pairs mated for life and each couple produced only one egg a year, laid in the open on the rocky ground.

Like many species, they were routinely hunted for food along the coasts by native peoples for centuries without having a serious impact on population numbers. With the dawn of the "Age of Exploration" increasing numbers of both the birds and their eggs were consumed by sea farers and colonists, and finally it was the demand for a luxury item that led their extinction.

Traditionally the down of the of the eider duck was used for pillows and quilts, but by the 16th century these ducks were hunted almost to extinction and the down of the great auk began to be used as a substitute. The fact that huge numbers of auks gathered in small areas during the nesting season made collection of their down a simple matter. Living birds were seized, stripped of their highest quality feathers, and discarded generally to die a lingering death.

The ultimate irony is that, as the last few birds faced the threat of imminent extinction, scientists, and naturalists madly raced to capture and kill the final few "specimens" for display in museums and private collections.

RECIPES:

Surviving accounts of cooking great auk are particularly horrible since they involve boiling the birds for soup or stews over a fire fueled by the bodies of the birds themselves, often while they were still living. The amount of fat stored on the birds was apparently sufficient for the purpose. No more sophisticated recipes appear to exist. The eggs of the great auk were also collected and usually eaten boiled.

CONSERVATION STATUS: EXTINCT.

The great auk is another of the species being considered for "de-extinction." Sufficient DNA can be collected from museum specimens and inserted into the eggs of the razorbill, its nearest relative, possibly resulting in recreating the species.

Yellow Breasted Bunting

The yellow breasted bunting, or rice bird, was up until the beginning of the 2000s, a widely distributed migratory bird routinely described as being "super abundant" and of "least concern" from a conservationist's point of view. Currently, it is being referred to as "the next passenger pigeon" as its population has declined, with incredible rapidity. Its population in Europe was estimated in 2004 to be between 60,000 and 300,000 individuals. As of 2015, there were estimated to be just 120 to 600 mature birds remaining. Similar declines have been observed across its range, which covers much of Europe, the Middle East, and Asia.

The yellow-breasted bunting is a small bird, ranging from 5.5 to 6.3 inches in length, and weighing less than an ounce. It migrates in large flocks from its breeding grounds in northern Europe and northern Asia to where it winters in south-east Asia, India and southern China, preferring to roost in rice fields. It was captured in huge numbers using fine mist nets during its migrations and on its wintering grounds. The birds were then shipped for consumption in the gourmet trade, primarily in China.

Although the population has been tremendously reduced in the past few years, they are still captured and consumed in areas where they survive.

RECIPE:

STEAMED YELLOW-BREASTED BUNTINGS AND CHINESE LIVER SAUSAGES ON RICE [From Foodno1 blog]

Ingredients:

150g night-fragrant flower
150g fish fillet
75g shrimps
75 g water chestnut
1 tbsp dark soy sauce
Dried mandarin orange peel
Ginger root

Seasoning
1 tbsp light soy sauce
1 tsp sugar
Pinch of sesame oil
3 tbsp broth

Marinade for the paddy sparrow
Ginger juice with a little wine
1 tsp light soy sauce
1 tsp sugar

Method
1. Clean the yellow-breasted buntings; soak and shred orange peel, shred the ginger. Put the peel, ginger and marinade into and over the birds and let stand.

2. Cook rice with two bowls of water. When water boils, turn down the heat. Cut liver sausage into 2 inch lengths and put on top of rice with the birds when the rice starts to bubble.

3. Cover and cook over high heat. Reduce heat when rice returns to the boil. Let the steam cook the birds slowly.

4. When the rice is done, pour the seasoning over the top and serve.

CONSERVATION STATUS: CRITICALLY ENDANGERED

There is a strong possibility of the yellow breasted bunting going extinct in the next few years.

Moa

Prior to its occupation by humans, sometime between 1250 and 1300 A.D., the group of islands that came to be known as New Zealand had been geographically isolated for around 80 million years. Like many remote islands, the area developed its own unique ecological system which, in this instance, was dominated by birds, many of which were flightless. Among these were several species of Moa, the largest of which reached 12 feet tall. Until the arrival of humans, the moa had only one predator, the truly gigantic Haast's eagle, which had a wingspan approaching 10 feet. It has been estimated that as many as 160,000 moa populated the islands at the time of the arrival of humans. Within 150 years, and possibly in a much shorter period of time, both the moa and the eagle that depended upon it as prey were extinct.

There is a large amount of archaeological evidence that humans both hunted moa and collected their eggs for food, and simply ate the species into extinction in an amazingly short period of time.

The process was helped along by a series of large fires, probably set by humans to clear land for agriculture, which destroyed much of the bird's forest habitat.

RECIPE:

Archaeological and linguistic evidence tends to indicate that the most common method of cooking moa was in the traditional Polynesian earth oven covered with leaves, as is still done to this day with pigs. The legs, being the most portable portions of the huge birds, seem to have been most commonly consumed.

A more modern recipe:

ground moa
1 sm. onion (chopped)
Moa Meat Loaf

1# 1 egg
1/2 c. applesauce or any grated fruit or veg.
3 slices bread (cubed)
3 Tblsp. water
1/2 tsp. Sea Salt
1/2 c. chopped mushrooms
Butter

GLAZE
1 Tblsp Honey
3 Tblsp Ketchup

Soak bread crumbs in water for 3 minutes. Mix all ingredients except glaze in large bowl. Mix well. Lightly butter inside of loaf pan. Pat mixture firmly into loaf pan. Bake in 375deg oven for 1 hour. Mix honey and ketchup. Place glaze on top of meatloaf. Continue cooking for 10 more minutes.

CONSERVATION STATUS: EXTINCT

There is considerable interest in bringing back the moa from extinction. A number of museum specimens exist and using tissue from this, the DNA sequence for one moa species has been determined. It is probable that attempts will be made shortly to resurrect the species, using the eggs of its present day relative, the emu, to host the embryos.

5. REPTILE RECIPES

Fig. 1. Le Cayman
Lézard-Crocodile.

Fig. 2.

According to the Reptile Database, in 2014 there were 10,038 reptile species, with new species being identified on a continuing basis. Unfortunately, as the Database report noted, many of the newly discovered species turn out to be endangered. As of September 2016, 196 reptile species were listed as critically endangered. These included 40 species of turtle, 7 species of crocodilians, 110 species of lizard and 39 species of snake.

With a few notable exceptions, reptile populations are declining worldwide, primarily resulting from habitat loss due to development and climate change. Collecting for the pet trade and hunting for food, sport, and to eliminate species seen as undesirable or dangerous, also take a large toll of reptiles.

Gopher Tortoise

Generic image of Tortoise

Native to the southeastern United States, the gopher tortoise is another "keystone species" whose existence is jeopardized by habitat loss, predation, and hunting by humans. A fairly large tortoise, with an average weight of 8.8 pounds, it digs extensive burrows that provide shelter for both itself and a wide range of other animals. Each tortoise builds several burrows covering as much as four acres. They commonly inhabit dry open woodlands and acquire virtually of their water from eating vegetation.

Humans have been hunting and eating gopher tortoises probably for as long as the two species have been neighbors, but as the human population of the southeast grew and increasing amounts of land were put under cultivation, pressure on the tortoise population increased. Not only were their burrows a hindrance to planting, but the animals themselves were considered to be quite tasty. It appears that in normal times, the effort required to dig out tortoises from their deep burrows limited the number taken, but this changed during the Great Depression when food of any sort was scarce and gopher tortoises were widely eaten under the sarcastic name of "Hoover chicken," after that president's campaign promise of "a chicken in every pot." For many folks the reality was tortoise stew when you could dig one out.

RECIPE

TORTOISE STEW

Recipes for gopher tortoise stew tended to vary widely depending on available ingredients. A typical recipe was published in the Smithsonian magazine.

Cut meat into 2-inch pieces and simmer in salted water until tender. In a large Dutch oven, fry some salt pork until crisp and the fat is rendered. Add meat and brown. Add a generous amount of chopped onion, some chopped bell pepper, minced garlic, diced tomatoes and simmer for 20 minutes.

Then add the water the meat was cooked in, some diced potatoes, a few bay leaves, salt and black pepper to taste, and a fresh datil pepper [a variety of hot red pepper] or a dash of datil pepper sauce. Simmer for 1½ to 2 hours over low heat. If necessary, thicken stew with a little flour dissolved in water, or some mashed hard-boiled egg yolks. Add a dash of sherry before serving.

Serve piping hot with rice and corn pone.

CONSERVATION STATUS: VULNERABLE.

Currently, all populations of gopher tortoises are considered vulnerable and several are endangered or already locally extinct. In Florida, at least, major conservation efforts are in effect and tortoises and their burrows are protected under state law with permits required to capture and relocate the tortoises.

Diamondback Terrapin

The terrapin is somewhat unique among turtles in that its natural habitat is the salt marshes along the Atlantic coast in that it is capable of moving freely between salt and fresh water. Female terrapin are larger than males, with shells averaging around 7 ½ inches compared to those of males which average about 5 inches. There have been concerns over terrapin populations for several decades, as their numbers have been in steady decline, with no improvement in sight. Currently, they seem to be in a sort of conservation limbo, with regulations varying from state to state regarding their level of protection. In some states they are considered endangered, while in others they are still considered fair game. The matter seems fairly political and appears to bear little relationship to the actual state of local populations.

Before most turtle populations were seriously depleted by "over-harvesting" for human consumption, turtle dishes and particularly turtle soup were immensely popular throughout

America. Of the several species that were used in recipes the diamondback terrapin was by far the most sought after.

Liner's *The Culinary Herpetologist* has a number of recipes for cooking terrapin as well as several dozen for preparing meals from whichever other species you have on hand. First you have to prepare the terrapin. If you have a reasonable degree of sensitivity, you might want to skip this part.

Keep terrapins for at least 1 week without feeding before killing by plunging into boiling salted water. Remove and strip off outer layer of skin. Return. Parboil for 1 ½ hours until the feet fall off and the shell cracks. Remove the turtle and place it on its back until cool enough to handle. Discard the heavy part of the intestines and gall bladder . Save the liver, heart, and eggs (if female) along with the meat. Pick to pieces and dice. The meat is then ready for various recipes.

RECIPE:

TERRAPIN SOUP

1 lb terrapin meat	4 med potatoes, chopped
½ gal milk	3 c onions, chopped
1 can of mushroom soup	6 stalks celery, chopped
1 lb mushrooms, chopped	24 ozs sour cream
2 tbsp dill chopped	2 tbsp basil, chopped
2 tbsp white pepper	2 tbsp beau monde seasoning
3 sticks butter	

Saute' the onions, potatoes, celery and mushrooms in the butter until tender. Let cool completely and then puree. Place in a large pot and add the remaining ingredients and cook over a medium heat. Watch carefully and stir often.

CONSERVATION STATUS: NEAR THREATENED to
ENDANGERED depending upon location.

A great many human activities endanger terrapins, since their primary habitat is in costal marshes and estuaries which are generally adjacent to ever increasing costal development. They are frequently killed by the propellers of recreational watercraft, hit by cars as they cross roads, caught and drowned in crab traps, run over by planes on airport runways, eaten by raccoons, and are victims of the continual process of habitat loss, both through filling of swamps and marshes and from flooding by rising sea levels.

Despite all of the above, it is still possible to buy your own baby terrapin over the internet, though at a relatively high price.

It seems likely that the diamond back terrapin will survive, if only in scattered remnant populations along the eastern Atlantic seaboard.

Komodo Dragon

The komodo dragon is the world's largest lizard, reaching ten feet in length and weighing as much as 300 pounds. It is one of around 79 species of monitor lizard native to Asia, Africa, Australia and various Pacific islands. In the wild, Komoto dragons are found on only five volcanic islands in Indonesia.

As a group, the monitor lizards have a very confusing conservation status, ranging from being commercially exploited for meat and leather in Indonesia and being considered an exotic invasive pest in the American south to receiving thorough protection in areas where the numbers of some species have been dangerously depleted.

RECIPES:

Monitor lizards are most commonly broiled over an open fire or baked in the ashes. The favorite part is the tail, which is very muscular and can be cooked without skinning or the necessity of cleaning out entrails, etc. The skin is easily removed after cooking.

The Culinary Herpetologist includes a somewhat more sophisticated recipe.

FRICASSEE OF KOMODO DRAGON

1 fat female monitor	butter
thyme	few small onions
1-2 bay leaves	parsley, chopped
Plain flour	water

Dress and cut up monitor into pieces, reserving the eggs. Brown the pieces in hot butter in a casserole. When browned, sprinkle a little flour over them. When this is browned, add a little water along with the parsley, bay leaf, thyme, and the onions. Simmer about 45 minutes. Add eggs and simmer a few minutes longer. Serve.

CONSERVATION STATUS: The Komodo Dragon is listed as a VULNERABLE species, with only about 3,000 individuals in the wild and a slowly declining population. The Komodo National Park was founded in 1980 largely to protect the species. It is comprised of the three larger islands, which host the largest populations of Komoto Dragons, and 26 smaller ones. A major problem relating to the survival of these large monitors is that they require large prey species upon which to feed, including wild pigs, deer and goats. On the smaller islands the prey species have become less common, probably due to poaching, resulting in serious declines in Komoto Dragons on those islands. In general, however, the species is likely to continue to survive as long as intensive conservation efforts on their native islands continue.

Timber Rattlesnake

The timber rattlesnake is a large, potentially quite dangerous pit viper found on the east coast of North America from New Hampshire to Northern Florida and westward from southern Minnesota down to east Texas. It favors wooded areas in higher locations with rock cliffs and ledges for sunning and hibernating. Formerly, it was fairly common and its range extended further north, but rattlesnakes and humans don't mix very well and it is extinct in Canada. Currently, it is extirpated (locally extinct) in Maine and Rhode Island, and endangered in Connecticut, Massachusetts, and Vermont. In New Hampshire, it is listed as critically imperiled, and considered the most endangered of any wildlife species in the state. Throughout most of the rest of its range it is considered either threatened or endangered.

Much of the former habitat of the timber rattlesnake has been developed for human use, their last refuge being some of the less accessible places of woods and rocks. Habitat loss, along with mortality on roads, and deliberate killing by humans seems likely result in the snakes being eliminated from most of their range in the immediate future.

RECIPES:

In the USA, rattlesnake is probably the most commonly eaten snake meat. Liner's *Culinary Herpetologist* has dozens of rattlesnake recipes, including the following.

CREOLE RATTLESNAKE

1 medium rattler, dressed	¾ cup plain flour
¼ cup butter	1 4 oz can mushrooms, sliced
1 cup white wine	1 8 oz can tomato sauce
½ tsp basil, ground	4 chicken bouillon cubes
1 onion, diced	2 bell peppers, diced
½ cup water	¼ cup cornstarch
Salt and pepper to taste	paprika to taste

Clean meat from the bones and cut into bite size pieces. Season flour with salt, pepper, and paprika. Dredge meat in flour and brown in butter. In a saucepan add the liquid from the mushrooms, wine, tomato sauce, basil and boullion; simmer 15 minutes. Stir in mushrooms, onion, peppers, and meat. Cover and cook over low heat for 30-45 minutes or until meat is tender. Combine cornstarch and water, and stir into creole until thickened. Serve over rice.

CONSERVATION STATUS: Although officially listed as a species of "LEAST CONCERN," it is Endangered, Threatened or Extirpated throughout much of its range. As its habitat continues to be lost to development and its elimination as a dangerous species remains the primary response to its presence near human habitations, its population is certain to continue in decline for the foreseeable future.

6. AMPHIBIANS

Amphibians are vanishing from the earth. In the past few decades so many species have gone extinct, and so many others are critically endangered, that experts are saying that this represents the largest loss of biodiversity recorded to date. Of the approximately 7,000 species of amphibians, close to 1,900 are threatened and 168 have recently gone extinct.

As of this writing there are 105 species of salamander considered endangered and 79 more as critically endangered. 737 species of frogs are endangered and another 466 critically so.

Habitat loss is a major factor in amphibian decline, but what is also decimating numerous species of frogs and salamanders is Chytridiomycosis is an infectious disease of amphibians caused by an aquatic fungal pathogen, *Batrachochytrium dendrobatidis.* The disease has a variety of symptoms, but the most common is a thickening of the skin which can disrupt the passage of nutrients and metabolic wastes and even prevent respiration.

The disease has spread rapidly around the world primarily through the agency of humans. Amphibians are traded globally, for pets, for human consumption – most commonly American bullfrogs – and for fishing bait. They are also transported accidentally along with produce, particularly bananas. For some critically endangered species, captive breeding programs may be the only hope for survival.

Achoques

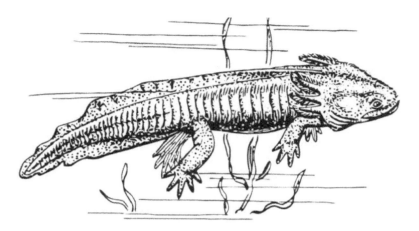

Salamander similar to Achoques

Achoques is the local name for the Lake Pátzcuaro Salamander, *Ambystoma dumerilii*. It is completely aquatic, being one of the few salamanders that does not normally metamorphose into a terrestrial form. In the wild it occurs only in one high altitude lake in Mexico. In the past it was fairly common and both eaten and used medicinally. Apparently it was so tasty that overfishing reduced the catch of them from 19 tons to zero in just 4 years. In addition to overfishing, the Achoques is endangered by pollution from untreated sewage discharge and from introduced predators.

In what has to be one of the more unusual conservation stories, although the species is on the verge of extinction – if not actually extinct – in the wild, one captive breeding population of about 400 individuals has been maintained for a number of years by a local convent of nuns. Traditionally the nuns have funded their operations by producing and selling a cough syrup made from locally caught Achoques. As the wild supply began to diminish, they brought some into the convent where they now maintain a sophisticated captive breeding program. It is hoped that if the environmental problems of Lake Pátzcuaro can be mitigated, eventually the salamanders could be reintroduced from the convent stock.

RECIPE

The salamander measures just 5 to 11 inches long and must be skinned and dressed before cooking, which is apparently no easy feat. Liner recommends nailing it to an upright post and peeling the skin off with a sharp knife and pliers.

ACHOQUES A LA VERACRUZANA

2 lbs Achoques, dressed
4 tbsp olive oil
¼ tsp cinnamon
3 tbsp capers
1 tsp salt
1 onion, chopped
¼ tsp cloves
1 tbsp lemon juice
1 clove garlic, crushed
5 tomatoes
1/3 c jalapeno pepper strips
1/3 c stuffed olives, halved

Rub Achoques with salt and garlic. Heat oil and add the onion and sauté for 5 minutes until soft and golden. Add the tomatoes (peeled, seeded, and chopped), cinnamon and cloves and simmer gently for 5 minutes. Place the Achoques in a buttered oven dish and cover with jalapeno peppers, capers, lemon juice and olives. Cover with the tomato mixture. Bake in preheated 350 degree oven for 30-40 minutes or until Achoques are tender. Serve with frijoles and crisp tortillas.

CONSERVATION STATUS: POSSIBLY EXTINCT IN THE WILD

The small breeding population maintained in captivity is vulnerable to any number of hazards despite the best efforts of its caretakers. Deleterious effects of inbreeding are likely now that the population can likely no longer be renewed by additional individuals taken from the wild.

Rice Field Frog

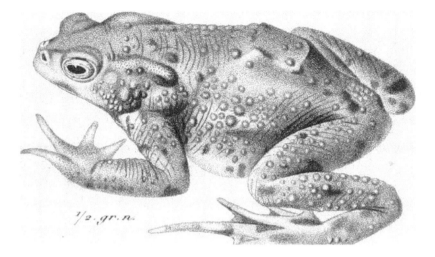

Each year, over 3 billion frogs, worth tens of millions of dollars, are eaten world-wide. Many of these are commercially raised, primarily in China, Taiwan, Ecuador and Mexico, with the American bullfrog the most commonly farmed species. Generally only the legs of these frogs are eaten.

While some farmed frogs are kept in semi-natural conditions, most are raised in horrendous factory-farms, densely packed in indoor facilities. In addition to these, vast numbers of frogs from a wide variety of species are also captured from "the wild" and consumed by humans or, in the case of exotic species, sold in the pet trade. The collection from the wild is of special concern since most frog populations are declining in number due not only to harvesting by humans but also to pollution, disease, habitat loss and degradation, as well as effects associated with climate change.

The Rice Field Frog, *Fejervarya limnocharis*, exemplifies many of the problems that all frogs face, and also the difficulties both of evaluating the conservation status of the species as a whole and in mitigating the factors that are threatening its existence.

The relatively small frog is widespread throughout much of South East Asia and Indochina. It generally is listed as a species of "least concern," but this designation disguises the fact that its populations in many areas are rapidly diminishing or already extinct. As the name implies, the frogs have always been common in rice paddies where the workers would collect them for a welcome addition to their diet. Their existence, however, is threatened in these environments by the toxic effects on their tadpoles of the application of Butachlor, the most commonly used herbicide in the rice fields. Damage to the species is also caused by a range of other agricultural pesticides and fertilizers, as well as pollution from existing and newly developed industries.

Aside from agricultural fields, the rice field frog is found in ponds, ditches, marshes, and even puddles. Many such areas are under threat from increased temperatures due to climate change. Others are drained in attempts to control mosquito borne diseases. Still others are eliminated to provide housing and food for the ever increasing human populations.

The vast area through which this frog occurs and the multiplicity and variety of habitats where it is found make it almost impossible to make any reasonably accurate estimate of its world-wide population size. What is apparent is that it is subject to all of the environmental dangers which are reducing amphibian populations everywhere, with the additional misfortune added of being eagerly sought after for human consumption.

RECIPE:

BETUTE – STUFFED FROG. [Traditional Philippine recipe]

Ingredients

8 big edible frogs (palakang bukid – rice field frogs)
1/4 kilos ground pork
3 cloves of minced garlic
1/2 teaspoon salt (for pork stuffing)
1 tablespoon vinegar (for pork stuffing)
1/2 teaspoon ground pepper (for pork stuffing)
1 teaspoon of salt (for marinade)
4 tablespoon of vinegar (for marinade)
1 teaspoon ground pepper (for marinade)
1 1/2 teaspoon brown sugar (for marinade)

Instructions
1. In a bowl, combine the ground pork, minced garlic, salt, vinegar, and ground pepper. Set aside.
2. Clean the frog and remove the skin and head, and cut the belly to remove the intestines.
3. Use the ground pork mixture as belly stuffing. Sew to prevent the stuffing's from spilling out.
4. Mix the marinating mixture: salt, vinegar, ground pepper, and brown sugar.
5. Pour into the stuffed frogs.
6. Let it stand for 30 minutes.
7. The let it sun-dry for another 30 minutes.
8. Deep fry until golden brown.
9. Serve with fried rice or steamed plain rice.

CONSERVATION STATUS: LEAST CONCERN

Although not officially considered endangered, many populations are declining or extirpated due to habitat loss, collection for food, pollution by a variety of agricultural chemicals, particularly the very widely used herbicide Butaclor, the effects of climate change on rice fields and other shallow freshwater frog habitat, and particularly *Batrachochytrium dendrobatidis,* the fungal pathogen that is devastating amphibian populations over an ever increasing area. Given its very widespread distribution and the frequency which suitable habitats occur even in urban areas, it is unlikely to go totally extinct in the near future, although its numbers may well be dramatically reduced.

Chinese Giant Salamander

The Chinese giant salamander (*Andrias davidianus*) is the both the largest salamander and the largest amphibian in the world, with the biggest recorded specimens reaching close to six feet long and weighing up to 140 pounds. It is considered to be one of two most critically endangered salamanders and the one that is in most in need of immediate conservation action. They once occurred in numerous locations throughout China, but now are almost extinct in the wild due to habitat destruction, pollution, and over-collection for both food and traditional Chinese medicine.

Samuel Turvey, of the Zoological Society of London, has stated, "The overexploitation of these incredible animals for human consumption has had a catastrophic effect on their numbers in the wild over an amazingly short time span. Unless coordinated conservation measures are put in place as a matter of urgency, the future of the world's largest amphibian is in serious jeopardy."

Giant salamanders are raised on a number of "farms" in China, which might normally be a hopeful sign for the survival of the species, however it is believed that many of the animals in these facilities have been illegally collected in the wild and simply and kept until they achieve maximum marketable size.

The status of the giant salamander has recently been complicated by the discovery that what was thought to be a single species is actually composed of at least five closely related species, meaning that each of these species is in far greater danger of extinction than previously thought.

RECIPES:

The giant salamander has been a traditional food and medicine in China for thousands of years. It is said to have a tender texture and taste rather like fish. It has a high nutritional value and is said to be useful in the treatment of many ailments, so much so that it has been called "live ginseng of the sea." The fact that it is now a critically endangered species has limited the availability of recipes using it as an ingredient, but the following patent, granted in China in 2012 describes the invention of a method of cooking the salamander. Note that no attempt has been made to edit the translation.

PATENT CN101779793B

The invention discloses a cooking method of giant salamander nourishing soup, belonging to cuisine cooking methods. The invention aim at providing the cooking method of the nourishing soup, and the nourishing soup has tender meat, delicious soup taste and rich nutrition and takes giant salamanders as main raw materials. The nourishing soup is cooked by the raw materials of the following main ingredients and subsidiary ingredients: a fish head and a fish tail of the giant salamander with the weight of 2.5 to 3.5 kilograms, a cock with the weight of 1 to 1.5 kilograms, as well as proper amount of ginger, monosodium glutamate, pepper and moderate common salt. The manufacturing method comprises the following steps of: butchering the giant salamander, removing internal organs, taking the finish head, and cutting the finish tail to diced meat for backup; butchering the cock and cutting the cock to meat lumps for stewing; and then adding the backup giant salamander head, the diced meat of the finish tail, the ginger, the monosodium glutamate, the pepper and the common salt, and boiling for 10 to 15 minutes with slow fire. The invention has the advantages of delicious and light soup taste, good nourishing effect, and the like, and the giant salamander nourishing soup is a delicious nourishing cuisine.

CONSERVATION STATUS: CRITICALLY ENDANGERED

The Chinese Giant Salamander has been designated as the amphibian most in need of conservation action.

7. FISH

SALMON FISHING.

Humans are a terrestrial species and the aquatic environment is alien to us, so much so that if we immerse ourselves in it completely for a matter of a few minutes, we die. What we know about its inhabitants and its ecological systems we have learned, correctly or incorrectly, from collections made remotely by fishing gear, from captive individuals in aquaria, and from relatively brief observational visits, generally into its most accessible parts. Members of our few expeditions to the deepest parts of the ocean have been far more restricted in their movements and contact with the environment than were our astronauts walking on the moon.

Our innate inability to live and work in the aquatic environment has made it very difficult both to evaluate the ecological systems and to determine the effects our increasingly indiscriminate harvesting of their component species. In reality, we still know very little about the life histories of many of the fish species which we consume for food and this, along with the intense politics surrounding the control of economically valuable fisheries, renders responsible decision making on conservation of individual species extremely difficult. In our rush to exploit new fish species to replace those whose stocks we have depleted, we are in danger of driving species like the deep sea "red roughy" into extinction before we know anything at all about them

Depending upon the source of the information, there are between 28,000 and 35,000 species of fish of which about 1,850 are in danger of extinction, including over a third of all sharks and rays. Overall, 3.0% of fish are critically endangered, including a number of very familiar species that humans have used as food for millennia.

Sturgeon

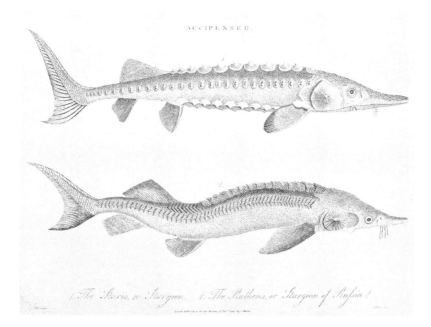

1. The Sturio, or Sturgeon. 2. The Ruthena, or Sturgeon of Russia.

The sturgeon has existed on earth for at least 200 million years. Currently there are 27 species of sturgeon, four of which may be extinct, and most of the remainder are critically endangered, at the very edge of extinction. As a whole sturgeon are considered to be one of the most threatened group of animals on the planet.

The two species which are of greatest commercial value, and therefore under greatest threat of extinction through direct human action, are the Atlantic sturgeon and the Beluga sturgeon. Both are extremely large and long-lived fish, reaching 14 or 15 feet and 60 to 100 pounds. Although their flesh is eaten, often as smoked sturgeon, they are most highly valued for their eggs – caviar. Beluga black caviar can sell for as much as several thousand dollars a pound. The fact that these sturgeon take 20 to 25 years to become sexually mature, and that the largest breeding females are the most desirable to catch, make recovery of the species in the wild almost impossible. Even with protected status, the great wealth that can be made from black market caviar sales results in continual poaching that puts further pressure on the already dangerously depleted populations. This is another case of a species being driven into extinction by the appetites of the rich for a product that no one actually needs to consume.

In addition to overfishing, a variety of other human created conditions have led to the destruction of sturgeon populations. All of the species are anadromous, living in salt water as adults and entering fresh water rivers to spawn. The construction of dams in most river systems has prevented sturgeon from reaching their traditional breeding grounds. In the remaining river areas they were quite vulnerable to commercial fishing operations, often being taken as by-catch and killed and discarded by fishermen.

In the Connecticut River, which historically saw vast spawning runs of a number of fish species, sturgeon often became entangled in nets set to catch shad and other river herring. Once ensnared, the sturgeon tended to thrash and roll, often wrecking the nets. If the sturgeon did not die in the nets, the fishermen would kill them as destructive nuisances. In addition to all of this, continuing development on shorelines has greatly reduced available spawning areas and runoff from sewage systems and large agricultural and industrial operations has seriously polluted many of the rivers.

RECIPES:

Russian Fish Kebabs

Ingredients

2 medium onions, finely chopped
2 large garlic cloves, finely chopped
1 jalapeño, finely chopped
1 fresh red chili, finely chopped
1 cup chopped dill
1 cup chopped parsley
1 cup dry white wine
4 pounds sturgeon cut into 2-inch pieces
Vegetable oil, for brushing
Salt and freshly ground pepper
Lemon wedges and grilled flatbread, for serving

In a large bowl, toss the onions with the garlic, jalapeño, red chile, dill, parsley and wine. Add the fish and stir to coat thoroughly with the marinade. Cover and refrigerate for 4 hours.

Light a grill. Thread the fish onto 8 metal skewers, leaving a small space between each piece. Brush the fish with oil and season with salt and pepper.

Grill over high heat, turning occasionally, until lightly charred and just opaque throughout, about 12 minutes.

Serve with lemon wedges and grilled flatbread.

CAVIAR: Sturgeon caviar is being produced in increasing quantities by more or less responsible aquaculture in a number of countries, but the price still remains prohibitively expensive. Reasonably priced alternatives can be found in many grocery stores and online. These most commonly include capelin caviar, which is died black to look like sturgeon roe, and salmon eggs which are larger and generally orange in color, and a number of others. They will do if you are not rich.

CONSERVATION STATUS: CRITICALLY ENDANGERED

85% of sturgeon species are at risk of extinction. In some areas habitat destruction and illegal fishing remain serious problems that might result in local extinction of populations, or even of entire species of sturgeon. In other locations, however, improvements in water quality, dam removal and improved protection is resulting in increased population sizes and even the return of fish to parts of their former territories from which they were previously extirpated. Increasingly large and successful sturgeon farming operations in a number of countries also are playing a major role in species preservation.

Tristramella Sacra

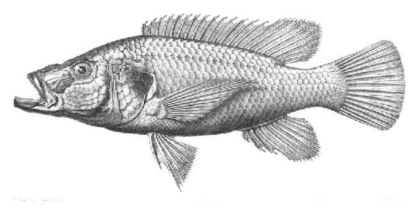

This fish, which apparently has no common name in English was endemic to the Sea of Galilee, also known as Lake Tiberias or Yam Kinneret, among other names. It is a cichlid fish, akin to the tilapia, growing to around 11 inches. It was one of the fishes which would have been captured in the nets of Saint Peter and his fellow Galilean fishermen. It has not been seen since 1990 despite very thorough searches and is believed to be extinct.

Like so many other species, *T. sacra* was the victim of climate change, but even more so of the overuse of water resources, primarily for agricultural purposes. The breeding area for this species was in the marshy areas in the north of the lake and these have dried out several times in recent years.   Lake Tiberias has been suffering from low water levels since it is used as a major source of water for both Israel and Jordan. The Jordan River which flows into the lake from the north is itself in danger of disappearing through excessive withdrawals of water. The Dead Sea, which is the southern terminus of the river has reached historically low levels and faces the possibility of vanishing completely

Recently, Israel has been greatly expanding its desalinization of sea water to provide for agricultural and domestic needs and has committed to a number of projects designed to increase the amount of water in the Jordan River system, but the ultimate results of these attempts is uncertain. Whatever the outcome, they will not come in time for *T. sacra* and the other life forms that have already become extinct through the destruction of their habitat in Lake Tiberias.

RECIPIES:

At the time of Christ many fishes from Lake Galilee would have been preserved by drying, salting, and or smoking. Those involved in the "loaves and fishes" story would, no doubt, have been preserved in one of these ways for a "picnic" lunch. At home they might have been cooked in a simple fish stew with onions and barley, as they were in ancient Egypt. The following is a more modern recipe.

SPICY FISH CAKES WITH PINE NUTS

Ingredients:

¼ cup pine nuts
1 lb filets of Tristramella sacra (or tilapia, a similar cichlid)
1 medium onion, minced
½ cup bread crumbs
1 large egg
½ tsp salt (or more to taste)
½ tsp cumin
¼ tsp cayenne (more or less to taste)
Olive oil for frying (medium heat)
Tahini sauce for dipping

Toast the pine nuts until golden in a small skillet
Coarsely chop the fish into very small pieces with a sharp knife
Place all ingredients in a large bowl and stir until well blended
Form mixture into small patties and fry until golden brown on
   on both sides.
Drain on paper towel and serve hot with tahini.

CONSERVATION STATUS: VERY PROBABLY EXTINCT

Nile Perch

The Nile Perch, *Lates niloticus,* is not itself an endangered species, rather it is an example of how the introduction of a commercially desirable species into a new environment can result in the extinction of the native fauna.   This species was one of a number of fishes that were exploited for food in ancient Egypt. It is a top tier predator, growing as large 2 m (6 ft 7 in) and 200 kg (440 lb). The illustration above, found it the tomb of the Vizier Kagemni, dates from around 2650 BC and shows men fishing from a papyrus reed boat, using a line with multiple hooks and scooping the catch into the boat with a landing net. Several species, including the Nile Perch are illustrated, and the number and variety of fish give an indication of the richness of the healthy, balanced river ecosystem that provided a large proportion of the food consumed by humans in Egypt for thousands of years.

The Nile Perch is a valuable food fish and also quite popular with anglers, because of its size and the fact that it can be caught on hook and line with artificial lures. Before humans had a clear understanding of the inter-relationship of the various organisms in an ecosystem, it was popular to introduce species favored by sportsmen and commercial interests into new environments, without thought to the ultimate consequences, which were often quite horrendous. Such was the case with the introduction of the Nile Perch into various enclosed bodies of water, including Lake Victoria, the second largest body of fresh water in the world, located between Kenya, Uganda and Tanzania.

Prior to the 1950s, Lake Victoria supported an incredibly diverse population of fishes composed of over 500 different species, many of which had evolved in the lake and occurred nowhere else on earth. After the introduction of Nile Perch at least 200 of these species became extinct and others were dramatically reduced in numbers, some surviving now only in aquaria. The Nile perch population expanded rapidly as did its fishery, with the number of fishing boats expanding from about 12,000 in 1983 to over 50,000 by 2004. Fishing craft also changed from traditional hand paddled canoes to larger gasoline powered vessels. So many vessels were on the lake, even in the worst weather conditions, that it was reported that about 5,000 people a year, mostly fishermen, lost their lives by drowning.

In the 1990s over 500,000 tons of Nile Perch from Lake Victoria were exported each year. The introduction of one extremely successful predator had in a very short period of time resulted in the total disruption of the ecosystem of the second largest lake in the world and the extinction of the majority of its indigenous fish species.

RECIPES:

Nile perch as it would have been served in Ancient Egypt.

NILE PERCH WITH FLAT BREAD

Ingredients:

2 lbs Nile Perch
1 medium onion
1 liter of water
2 tablespoons of oil
1 dried and ground lemon
1 teaspoon of salt
1/2 teaspoon of pepper
2 loaves of flat bread

Preparation:

Scale and gut the fish. Wash the fish well with cold water. Chop the onion into cubes and fry in oil until golden. Add water and bring to a boil.

Season the fish with salt, pepper, and ground lemon powder and then add the fish to the boiling water.

After ten minutes take the fish from boiling water and remove bones. Reserve the broth.

Soak the flat bread in the broth and serve with the fish.

CONSERVATION STATUS: THRIVING – to the detriment of many other species.

Sharks

The earliest ancestors of the sharks evolved over 440 million years ago and over time diverged into a large number of species, about 535 of which are alive today. The total number of sharks killed annually by humans, as well as the number killed of each individual species is extremely difficult to determine. Detailed catch records are generally not kept, since sharks are considered to be of little market value, and those that are kept do not identify the sharks caught by species. Additionally, many sharks are killed only for their fins and their bodies discarded, while many are simply killed for sport, because of irrational fear, or out of unthinking destructiveness. The issue is further complicated by the wide variety of shark species, many of which are difficult to distinguish from one another.

Recent studies have estimated that at least one quarter of sharks, and their close relatives rays and chimeras, are threatened by overfishing. These are generally the large species that live in shallower waters accessible to fishermen.

Other more obscure species, such as the eight inch long dwarf lantern shark, may also be at risk, but their population trends are difficult to evaluate. For most sharks and rays, fishing is being carried out without yield targets or any sort of regulation, and strong evidence exists that while catch numbers show only modest reduction, in actuality large "most desirable" species have been seriously overfished and their numbers replaced in the statistics by smaller, "less desirable" species. In short, a familiar pattern emerges where the large top level predators are selectively removed by humans, throwing an entire ecosystem out of balance with unpredictable, but often very destructive results.

Most recently, there has been a dramatic increase in the hideous practice of catching and "finning" sharks – cutting off their fins for use in gourmet shark fin soup and throwing the still living fish overboard to die a slow cruel death. Such attempts that are made to outlaw the practice are commonly ignored.

RECIPES:

In 1993, Marine Biologist Russ Lockwood, wrote *Fish Cookery*, which included recipes for a wide variety of fishes, including a number of sharks. At that time no one conceived that sharks, which were common in the seas around the world, were in any danger of extinction. He notes that "most sharks are good to eat, usually tasting rather like a swordfish, but they require special care because of their peculiar biology. Modern fish regulate osmotic pressure by a kidney, but sharks are primitive and carry uric acid in their blood for osmotic balance. The acid breaks down very quickly after the fish dies, releasing ammonia into the blood. So sharks must be bled and eviscerated at once if they are to be eaten."

SHARK CASSEROLE

Ingredients

¾ cup chopped celery
½ cup chopped onion
1 chicken bullion cube
¼ cup (1/2 stick) butter or margarine
2 teaspoons cornstarch
1 cup whole milk
2 cups chopped mixed vegetables
1 tablespoon chopped fresh parsley
Pinch of pepper
1 cup chopped cooked shark meat
1 package refrigerator rolls

Procedure

Preheat oven to 350 degrees F. Place celery, onion, bullion cube, and butter in a microwave safe dish. Cover with perforated plastic wrap or a paper towel to prevent spattering, and microwave on high for about 2 minutes or until onion and celery are soft; or saute' them on top of the stove.

Combine the cornstarch and milk in a medium saucepan. Add the vegetables, parsley, and pepper. Cook over medium heat, stirring constantly, to thicken sauce, about 10 minutes.

Stir the onion mixture and flaked fish into the sauce. Pour into a medium baking dish. Break apart rolls and put on top of the casserole. Bake for about 20 minutes, or until the casserole is golden brown and bubbly.

TRADITIONAL SHARK FIN SOUP

From: *"The Chinese Cook Book," by Shiu Wong Chan of New York, 1917. Pages 101-102.)*

(a) Buy dry shark fins from Chinese grocery store. Soak in cold water for 3 hours.

(b) Boil fins with several pieces of dry garlic and 2 pieces of ginger root. Change water several times when boiling.
(c) Put into pan. Add 2 tablespoonfuls of lard, and more than twice the amount of primary soup to cover. Boil slowly for ½ hour. Drain off the liquid and throw it away.
(d) Put into another pan with 6 pints of primary soup. Boil.
(e) Change again into third pan of primary soup. Add gravy (1 cup of chicken starch, whites of 3 eggs, diced Chinese ham and a little cornstarch and salt). Use 1 tablespoonful red vinegar to improve taste. Garnish with parsley. Serve hot.

IMMITATION SHARK FIN SOUP

Ingredients

2 shiitake mushroom(s)	1 tbsp soy sauce
10 scallops (dried)	1 tsp salt
4 tbsp Korean glass noodles	0.5 tbsp dark soy sauce
1.2 l water	2 tbsp corn flour
1 chicken drumstick	1tbsp water
1 black fungus/mu-er mushroom	0.5 tsp white pepper
2 tsp crab meat	1 egg
1 tbsp shaoxing wine	0.5 tsp white pepper

Preparation:
1. Hydrate dried shiitake mushrooms, wood ear mushroom and Korean glass noodles in-room temperature water until soft. In a pot, boil water and allow it to simmer along with drumstick and dried scallops for an hour. Then, remove drumstick and scallops from broth and shred them.
2. Boil broth at medium to high heat. Add shredded drumstick, scallops, crab meat, sliced wood ear mushrooms, sliced shiitake mushrooms, Shaoxing wine and soy sauce. Boil for 10 minutes.
3. Thicken with corn flour dissolved in a little water. Add pepper to taste.

4. Beat an egg and carefully pour it into soup. Turn stove off after 10 seconds. Serve with some Chinese black vinegar and a few drops of sesame oil.

CONSERVATION STATUS: THREATENED

Only one third of all sharks and rays are considered safe from extinction in the near future.

Eels

Eels.

Soon there may be no more eels.

Throughout human history in many parts of the world, the eel has provided an abundant and relatively inexpensive, high quality food source. The most commonly eaten species are those in the genus *Anguilla,* particularly the American, European, and Japanese eels. All of these species have seen their populations in the wild fall by at least 90% and possibly as much as 98% in the last few decades and all are considered endangered. While changing ocean conditions have had a significant effect in reducing eel populations, the most obvious cause is overfishing, much of it illegal, to supply both adult and young eels for human consumption, primarily in Japan, which annually utilizes in excess of 100,000 tons of the fish for food.

The eel has one of the most unusual and still mysterious life cycle of any fish. Unlike salmon, river herring and other fish that live in the sea and enter fresh water to breed, the eel lives most of its life in fresh or brackish water and breeds in the ocean. The traditional scientific belief is that all of the eels both from North America and Europe swim out to the Sargasso Sea, a distinct section of the North Atlantic, between North America and Africa, that is formed by four major ocean currents, all of which move in a clockwise direction. After breeding in this area, a phenomenon that is assumed, but has never actually been observed, huge numbers of young are produced, which ultimately are carried by the currents back to the coasts and the freshwater rivers in which they grow and mature. It can take between 10 to 25 years for an eel to mature and return to sea to breed and die.

American and European eels face two gigantic threats, human greed and the results of climate change. As the numbers of eels declines rapidly, so does the value of the remaining stock, particularly of "glass eels," the young eels arriving at the coastal rivers after their journey from the Sargasso Sea. These are collected both to serve as food and as stock for eel farming facilities, primarily in Japan. Since it is not possible to artificially fertilize adult eels or breed them in captivity, farming eels requires catching wild juveniles. As of this writing, a pound of live glass eels is worth thousands of dollars and there is a thriving business in eel poaching and smuggling. The fact that it takes a female eel at least 10 years to become capable of producing eggs makes the rapid replacement of a depleted population nearly impossible.

Perhaps even more destructive to eel populations is the increasing probability that there will be significant changes in ocean circulation patterns brought about by global warming. Since the young eels rely upon the established pattern of ocean currents to get them to their adult habitat, a collapse of a current like the Gulf Stream could spell disaster for the species.

RECIPES:

Jellied eel is a traditional British working class dish, particularly in the East End of London. "Eel, pie and mash shops" were, until recently, quite common in the city however, the recent crash of the eel population along with the great increase in their market price has made the meal unaffordable for many of their customers. Eel contains a great deal of gelatin, so the liquid in which they are cooked will gel upon cooling.

INGREDIENTS:

3 pounds fresh eel, peeled, cleaned and cut into 2" pieces
¼ cup malt vinegar
1 medium sized onion, thinly sliced
12 whole black peppercorns tied in a cheesecloth packet
2 small bay leaves
¼ cup fresh lemon juice
2 tbsp finely chopped parsley
2 tsp salt
2 ½ cups water
2 hard cooked eggs for garnish

Wash the pieces of eel thoroughly under cold running water.
Place the pieces of eel in salt water and let it soak for 5 minutes.
Rinse well under cold running water, then place the eel in a heavy 4- to 5-quart stainless-steel or enameled saucepan.
Add vinegar, sliced onion, peppercorns, bay leaves, salt and water, and bring to a boil over high heat.
Reduce the heat to low, cover the pan, and simmer for 20 minutes.
Transfer the pieces of eel to an baking dish (8x12x2-inch) With a slotted spoon, and stir the lemon juice into the cooking liquid. Discard the peppercorns.
Pour the entire contents of the pan over the eel, spreading the onion slices on top with a fork.

Sprinkle evenly with the parsley, and refrigerate for at least 4 hours. When thoroughly chilled, the liquid should form a soft jelly.

Cut eggs crosswise into 1/4-inch slices and arrange them attractively on the jelly and serve directly from the bowl.

Serves 4-6

CONSERVATION STATUS: CRITICALLY ENDANGERED

Extinction of American, Japanese, and European eels is highly probable in the near future. Extreme conservation methods, including the complete banning of the capture and consumption of adult and juvenile eels, should be enacted worldwide immediately. Changes in ocean currents, as a result of global warming, however, might render the best conservation efforts useless.

Codfish

For centuries, the cod was the most commercially important fish in the western world. The history of the cod fishery is long and complicated, stretching from the Viking days, through the collapse of the Northwest Atlantic cod population in 1992, which devastated the economy of Newfoundland, up to the present day when the cod has gone from occurring in shoals so thick one could hardly row a boat through them to the threshold of extinction.

For centuries, cod were caught by strong men line fishing by hand from sail or oar powered wooden boats. Millions of fish were caught off the American coast and consumed at home or exported, in the form of salt cod, to Europe or to feed the enslaved population of the Caribbean Islands. The fact that cod were a high protein food that could be preserved for long periods of time by salting and/or drying made it tremendously popular in the days before refrigeration or freezing. Yet the traditional fishing methods of the sort described in Rudyard Kipling's *Captains Courageous* though intensive were still sustainable. Moreover, they were selective, primarily catching only the valuable cod without depleting populations of other species, and they were gentle on the environment, since hook and line fishing does not significantly disrupt sea bed communities.

Beginning in the 1950s a sequence of technological innovations including radar, sonar, greatly improved trawling techniques, and electronic navigation systems culminated in the creation of super-trawlers that could fish longer, deeper, and more effectively than any in history. Catches increased tremendously, far exceeding the capacity of the cod population to reproduce sufficiently to replace the losses. According to statistics reported in the journal *Ecological Applications*, approximately 8 million tons of cod were caught between 1647 and 1750 (103 years), a period encompassing 25 to 40 cod generations. The factory trawlers took the same amount in 15 years.

Catches continued to grow until in 1968 landings of cod peaked at over 800,000 tons then began declining until the whole fishery crashed dramatically in 1992. Basically, the super-trawlers had become so numerous and so efficient that they had managed to catch virtually all the cod.

If that was not bad enough, the trawlers were not selective in their catch and the "by-catch" of other fish caught in the nets along with the cod devastated the stocks of a number of other species. The nets which fished along the ocean bottom also seriously harmed the communities of bottom dwelling organisms, maximizing the disruption of the ocean ecosystem. Even with severe restrictions on the fishery, stocks of cod have not recovered as expected.

RECIPE:

CODFISH CAKES

Ingredients

1 lb skinless boneless salt cod
1 medium onion, finely chopped
3 1/2 tablespoons unsalted butter
1 lb russet potatoes
1 parsnip
1/2 teaspoon black pepper
1 large egg, lightly beaten
1/2 cup plain dry bread crumbs
3 tablespoons vegetable oil

Preparation

Soak cod in a large bowl with cold water to cover by 2 inches, chilled, changing water 3 times a day, 1 to 3 days

Drain cod and transfer to a 3- to 4-quart pot with fresh water to cover by 2 inches. Bring just to a simmer and remove from heat. (Cod should just flake; do not boil, or it will become tough.) Drain in a colander.

Cook onion in 1/2 tablespoon butter in a 10-inch heavy skillet over moderate heat, stirring occasionally, until pale golden, about 7 minutes. Transfer to a large bowl.

Peel potatoes and parsnip. Halve parsnip lengthwise and remove core if tough. Cut potatoes and parsnip into 1-inch pieces and steam together in a steamer over boiling water in a large pot, covered, until tender, 18 to 20 minutes. Add to cooked onions and coarsely mash, then cool slightly. Flake cod stir into potato mixture along with salt to taste and pepper. Stir in egg until just combined.

Put bread crumbs in a shallow baking dish.

Form rounded 1/4-cup scoops of cod mixture into 12 (3-inch-diameter) cakes and transfer to a sheet of wax paper. Gently dredge fish cakes in bread crumbs to coat and transfer to a wax-paper-lined tray. Chill, covered with plastic wrap, at least 30 minutes.

Preheat oven to 200°F.

Heat 1 tablespoon butter and 1 tablespoon oil in 10-inch heavy skillet over moderate heat until foam subsides. Cook fish cakes, turning over once, until golden brown, 7 to 8 minutes total.

CONSERVATION STATUS: VULNERABLE

Some populations are endangered. Overfishing has seriously depleted populations to the point where previous prey species, such as the capelin, have increased tremendously in number to the point where they have become major predators on the eggs and young of the cod, further reducing the possibility of species recovery.

8. ARTHROPODS

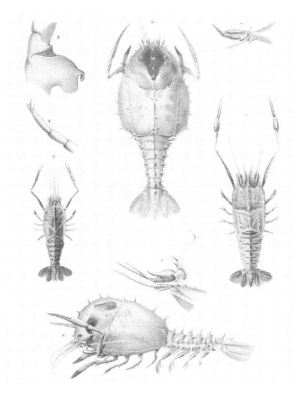

Arthropods are animals lacking a backbone, having an external skeleton, a segmented body, and jointed appendages. The four major groups of arthropods are insects, arachnids, myriapods (millipedes, centipedes and their relatives), and crustaceans. They are considered to be the most successful group of animals on earth and make up over 75% of all known living and fossil organisms. The International Union for the Conservation of Nature (IUCN) currently lists 6.5% of all species which have been evaluated as endangered.

Despite the vast number of arthropods, for reasons of space, only one species is considered here – the Horseshoe crab.

Horseshoe Crab

The horseshoe crab first appeared on earth some 450 million years ago and has remained substantially unchanged since that time. There are four existing species which live and breed in shallow coastal waters on the Atlantic and Gulf Coasts of North America and the coasts of Japan, Indonesia, India and elsewhere in Asia. Spawning generally takes place near beaches during Spring high tides, when a female may release between 60,000 and 120,000 eggs in a number of different batches. These eggs are a vital food resource for many species of migratory birds, including the red knot, which depends entirely on them for food during its migrations. Sea turtles and numerous species of fish also feed on the eggs. It has been speculated that without the horseshoe crab the ecosystem of the Atlantic shoreline from the Carolinas south would collapse.

This ancient, vital, and quite unique creature is currently under threat of from several distinct human related causes which together may ultimately drive it to extinction.

In America, while the horseshoe crab is rarely eaten itself, for many years they have been caught and used for bait to catch more desirable species, including eels and whelk (conch). Treating the crab as an easily collected "junk species," a vast number of them are cut up for bait annually, without a thought, until recently, of the consequences of their destruction.

An even greater threat has appeared recently with the discovery that their unique blue, copper based, blood can play an important role in human medicine, being used to test the sterility of drugs and medical devices. In 2016, more than 400,000 horseshoe crabs were captured and subjected to having a portion of their blood removed in the laboratory, after which they were released "alive" in the area from which they were taken. At least 10% to 15% of the animals die in the bloodletting process, plus an unknown number afterwards in the sea.

Research is currently underway, with some degree of success, to find less destructive alternatives to using the horseshoe crab for both these purposes.

Additionally, development along the shorelines, which continues unabated, reduces the area available to the crabs for spawning.

Finally, although the horseshoe crab rarely appears on menus in America, the eggs of the females are considered a delicacy and an aphrodisiac in various parts of Asia.

RECIPE:

The most basic way of serving horseshoe crab roe is to grill the entire animal, then lay it on its back and eat the eggs with a spoon. Somewhat more aesthetically appealing presentations can be made by boiling the crab for about 3 minutes then removing the roe once it has cooled. It can then be used in traditional recipes like

THAI HORSESHOE CRAB EGGS IN SPICY SALAD

Ingredients

1 cup steamed horseshoe crab eggs
1/2 cup shredded green mango
1 tbsp. thinly sliced shallot
1 tsp. thinly sliced chillies
1/2 tbsp. lime juice
1 tbsp. fish sauce
1/2 tsp. sugar

Toss the horseshoe crab eggs, mango, shallot, and chillies, seasoning with the lime juice, fish sauce, and sugar to taste, and then serve.

CONSERVATION STATUS: VULNERABLE

Considering the vital importance of the horseshoe crab to the ecosystem of much of the east coast of the United States, it is imperative that exploitation of the species both for use as bait and in human medicine be prohibited immediately. If this is done, there is a high probability that the species could make a good recovery. If the current level of exploitation is allowed to continue, the current severe decline in population numbers will continue, leading to the possible extinction of a species that has survived all environmental changes and challenges for 450 million years. If this should happen, it is inevitable that a number of other species will be drawn into extinction in its wake.

9. Recipe for Renewal

It is becoming increasingly clear that our planet is rapidly heading towards an environmental catastrophe the like of which has not occurred for many millions of years. The latest projections warn that the earth could warm by a "terrifying" 6 to 7 degrees Celsius by the end of the century. This coupled with the ever increasing loss of biological diversity, as species go extinct at an ever increasing rate, will inevitably lead to the collapse of ecosystems across the entire Earth.

Overwhelming scientific evidence indicates that the driving force behind the current crisis is both the tremendous over-consumption of the Earth's resources by humans, particularly the overuse of fossil fuels, and the ever increasing habitat destruction resulting from industrial agriculture and the extractive industries.

The evidence also predicts that amount of time remaining in which to mitigate the very worst of the damage is rapidly approaching zero.

Most of the recent statements on slowing and/or reversing climate change focus on the vital need to dramatically reduce our use of fossil fuels – oil, coal, fracked gas – and this certainly is true. Realistically speaking, however, we cannot stop the use of fossil fuels quickly without disrupting the entire economy of the world. We can eventually replace most of the uses, but that will take decades to complete entirely. Hundreds of millions of homes in the global north would have to be individually converted to renewable heating sources and over one billion petroleum fueled cars and trucks would need to be taken off the roads. This work has been begun and must continue at a vastly accelerated pace but, by itself, it cannot be completed in time to save us.

Many of the proposed solutions also focus primarily on actions to be taken by government or large corporations and minimize, or even ridicule the idea that the actions of individuals can be effective in producing major change. In reality, nothing could be further from the truth. Make no mistake about it. The majority of politicians and businesses are not going to take serious action against climate change unless they are forced to do so.

Even the best of the politicians cater to a variety of special interests which they feel can affect their electoral chances. They tend to go after the big, obvious climate criminals, while not seriously addressing the myriad of smaller players who collectively also contribute greatly to the problem. Only by making climate activists a major "special interest" in their own right, capable of swinging elections, will our representatives be convinced to actually represent our interests and those of the planet.

The multinational corporations are only concerned with their profits. Since ultimately those profits come from the pockets of the individual consumers, coordinated consumer behavior on a massive scale can, and must, affect how they address the climate crisis.

Given the impossibility of governments and corporations, even with the best of intentions, rapidly ending the dependence on fossil fuels, it falls to us as individuals and as an activist movement to determine a means by which we can buy time, a way of immediately and dramatically reducing greenhouse gas emissions and reversing habitat destruction while other larger scale solutions are being devised and implemented. In short we must immediately take those actions which are possible to do quickly and can produce the most significant results with the minimum possible disruption of society.

There is only one major source of both greenhouse gas emissions and habitat destruction that could be quickly reduced to a fraction of its current level without causing civilization to come to a halt, one action in which every individual could take part without having to freeze in winter, to starve for want of food, be unable to travel to work, or risk danger of arrest for defying the authorities – livestock production.

Currently livestock production uses about 30% of the earth's entire land surface, both as pasture and as the 33% all arable land which is used to produce feed for livestock. This works out to the fact that livestock industries utilize 83% of all farm land to produce only 13% of the calories used as the food used by humans. Cattle production is also a major driver of deforestation, particularly in the Amazon, where 70% of recently cleared forest land is being used for grazing.

World-wide, there are about 1.5 billion cows and bulls. On average each of these releases between 70 and 120 kilograms of methane a year, a gas which is 23 times more powerful as a greenhouse gas than carbon dioxide. All together this represents the equivalent of two billion metric tons of CO_2 per year.

In short two of the most serious causes of the climate/ extinction crisis are being driven to a great extent by the livestock industries.

The inescapable conclusion is that if we are to avoid the worst effects of the planetary catastrophe, the only possible alternative is that we must immediately and dramatically reduce the production and consumption of all animal products. Ideally large numbers of humans switching to an entirely plant based diet would produce the most significant impact, however experts more realistically suggest that reducing consumption by 80%, with the largest reduction being made in cattle farming, would produce tremendous results, among which would be a significant reduction in greenhouse gas production and the freeing up 60% of present pasture land for habitat restoration.

If we can reduce production and consumption of animal products to 20% or less of the current level worldwide, starting immediately, and reaching the 20% goal within the next three years, then we can gain much needed time to complete the conversion to renewable energy. If we cannot, then there is little hope for the continuation of the world as we have known it.

This process must begin immediately and the only place it can realistically begin is with each individual person. In a very real sense it will be a test. If we, and millions of others, can take the simple step of moving to a largely plant based diet, than we might actually manage to muster the will and the power to save our planet. If we cannot do even that, then we are lost.

BIBLIOGRAPHY

Apicius. Vehling, Joseph Dommers translator. 1936. *Cookery and Dining in Imperial Rome.* Reprint 1977. New York: Dover Publications.

Brennan, Jennifer. 2000. *Trade Winds and Coconuts: A Reminiscence & Recipes from the Pacific Islands.* Boston: Tuttle Publishing.

Chambers, Paul. 2004. *A Sheltered Life: The Unexpected History of the Giant Tortoise.* London: John Murray.

Davidson, Alan. 2003. *North Atlantic Sea Food: A Comprehensive Guide with Recipes.* Berkeley, California: Ten Speed Press.

Leipoldt, C. Louis. 1976. *Leipoldt's Cape Cookery.* Cape Town and Johannesburg, S. Africa: W. J. Flesch & Partners.

Le Guat, Francois. 1708. Facsimilie. *A new voyage to the East-Indies by Francis Leguat and his companions. Containing their adventures in two desart islands, ... Adorn'd with maps and figures.* London: British Museum.

Liner, Ernest A. 2005. *The Culinary Herpetologist.* Salt Lake City, Utah: Bibliomania!

Lockwood, Russ. 1993. *Fish Cookery.* New York: Lyons & Burford.

MacPhee, Ross D. E. and Peter Schouten. 2019. *The End of the Megafauna: The Fate of the World's Hugest, Fiercest, and Strangest Animals.* New York: W. W. Norton & Compant.

May, R. J. 1984. *KaiKai Aniani: a Guide to Bush Foods, Markets and Culinary Arts of PaPua, New Guinea.* Bathurst, N.S.W., Australia: Robert Brown & Associates.

Rorer, S. T. 1886. *Philadelphia Cookbook.* Philadelphia: Arnold and Company.

Simmons, Peter Lund. 1859. *The Curiosities of Food; or the Dainties and Delicacies of Different Nations Obtained from the Animal Kingdom.* London: Richard Bentley.

Simmons, Peter Lund. 1885. *The Animal Food Resources of Different Nations, with Mention of Some of the Special Dainties of Various People Derived from the Animal Kingdom.* London: E. & F. N. Spon.

Steller, Georg Wilhelm. 1751. Reprint 2011. *De bestiis marinis or, The Beasts of the Sea.* Lincoln Nebraska: Zea Books.

Walther, Michael and Julian P. Hume. 2016. *Extinct Birds of Hawaii.* Honolulu, Hawaii: Mutual Publishing, LLC.

About the Author

At the Dead Sea

Michael Westerfield has a master's degree in environmental science. He has worked as a Marine Biologist, studied Archaeology and Anthropology, and was director of a public housing authority for over twenty years. His two previous books are *The Language of Crows,* a study of the language, culture and natural history of the American crow, and *The Road to the Poorhouse,* the history of the poorhouse system in Connecticut. He alternates between pessimism and cautious optimism regarding the future of planet Earth.